GOD, SOUL, REINCARNATION, KARMA
A SPIRITUAL JOURNEY

MARY L. EASTLAND

GOD, SOUL,
REINCARNATION, KARMA
A Spiritual Journey

Copyright © 2015 Mary L. Eastland
ALL RIGHTS RESERVED

First Printing – March 2015
ISBN: 978-0-9961106-2-4 *(pb)*

NO PART OF THIS BOOK MAY BE REPRODUCED IN ANY FORM, BY PHOTOCOPYING OR BY AN ELECTRONIC OR MECHANICAL MEANS, INCLUDING INFORMATION STORAGE OR RETRIEVAL SYSTEMS, WITHOUT PERMISSION IN WRITING FROM THE COPYRIGHT OWNER/AUTHOR.

Printed in the United States of America on acid-free paper

Published by Mosaic Design Book Publishers
www.mosaicdesignbookpublishers.com
Dearborn, Michigan USA

You asked yourself, "Who am I?"
And your heart said, "I don't know."
But your soul insists that, "You are He."
So you looked to Me and said,
"Is it true that I am You?"
"Do you hear Me in the brook
Whose waters dance and swirl?"
"Oh yes, and in the sea
Whose billows break against the sand."
"And do you feel Me in the breeze
That sways the leaves upon My trees?"
"Yes, and in the winds that bring the storm
And in the calm that follows.
And in the warmth of the morning sun
And the soft caress of a gentle rain.
"And what of the colors that paint the sky?
And the vistas that unfold before you?
And things seen only in a beautiful dream?
And the loved ones who surround you?"
And as I gazed upon His grace
I lowered my eyes and said, "Yes, I see."

—Mary L. Eastland

GOD, SOUL, REINCARNATION, KARMA

A SPIRITUAL JOURNEY

It has been said that just one of every one thousand individuals seeks truth. And that of every one thousand who do seek, just one is able to find. That's *one in a million*.

If I were to pinpoint just when my religious concerns began, I would say it was in my early teens. I am now a septuagenarian. If I were to say exactly what motivated my doubt in what the church was telling me, it would be the instruction that anyone living before the time of Jesus was not saved—by the blood of Christ—which meant that they would not see Heaven which meant, by inference, they were destined for Hell. If you are not going to Heaven then you must be going to Hell, right? And we all know what that means: eternal torment to an unimaginable degree. "This is just not fair," I thought. "People who lived before the time of Jesus Christ were souls made in the image of God, just as the people who have lived since the time of Jesus Christ. Many if not most of the early people believed in God after some fashion and lived godly lives. Why should they not be allowed to go to Heaven? And as far as Hell goes, it is just not something that God would ever consider much less implement. The idea is un-godlike. I am a mere human, and I could not impose that fate on anyone for any reason."

If I were to pinpoint what tweaked my concerns and jump-started my active quest for truth, it would be when I discovered that theologians claim that Adam appeared in the Garden of Eden a mere six thousand years ago. Well, this can't be. Even the late-comer, Cro-Magnon man, appeared about thirty thousand years ago in France. Just where did the Bible "scholars" get their information anyway? If the six-thousand-year figure is correct, I had to prove it for myself. So began my efforts either to disprove or to substantiate this important bit of information.

I pursued many avenues of thought and did a lot of reading. I also did a lot of meditating and spent a lot of time praying for direction. In addition to the use of varied treatments on the subject, I relied on two books in particular: *The Authorized (King James) Version of the Holy Bible* (the protestant Christian bible) and the *New World Translation of the Holy Scriptures* (the Jehovah Witness bible). Long story short, according to these two books, Adam did appear on the earthly scene circa 4000 B. C., a mere six thousand years ago. Bible references that support this fact are presented in my book *Genesis: A Tale Twice Told*. What that does to the claim that Adam was the first man on Earth, as my church encouraged me to believe, you will have to determine for yourself. For me, it put an end to that story. In my quest for that truth, I inadvertently discovered an even more important one. By their worship of the god of the Old Testament, Christians are most assuredly worshipping a false god.

This book is a result of my unfolding search for truth. It will follow what I believe to be the natural and necessary progression of one's quest for spiritual understanding. That progression, as shown here, will unfold as individual topics: specifically, God, soul, reincarnation, and karma.

Please keep in mind that what you will read here is my own interpretation, understanding, and acceptance of various belief systems that have blended and congealed to form my own personal beliefs. Each individual must find his or her own path to truth, and the paths are numerous and varied. However, there are certain protocols that I believe are necessary if truth is to be found.

To begin with, one must believe in God. Regardless of the name you give to the entity that you perceive to be God, you must realize that there is a God and that there is but one God. A single creative force or intelligence—I call it essence—is responsible for everything that exists. This essence, this "God" created man and woman and all else in existence. We do not know the process or means by which this was accomplished or the timeframe involved. It does not matter that we do not know. One might pursue this mystery as a matter of interest but must understand that he will never discover the definitive answer.

In the beginning, God ordained that there would be an infinite number of material bodies and various objects moving and orbiting throughout the cosmos. He ordained that some of these bodies would support physical life. He ordained that one of these bodies, which came to be called Earth, would house a particular living creature that came to be called man. He ordained that man would rise above and dominate all other living creatures and life forms on Earth.

Life really did begin as a miracle. For man, it began when two cells of like nature but different designations called gametes or germ cells came together, initializing active growth. In this early stage, the organism is referred to as a zygote and then continues through the stages of embryo and fetus. These, of course, are man's terms for his own development. These earliest stages of life took place in a liquid environment. As the organism reached an adequate stage of growth and development, it moved from its watery environment into a gaseous one by the process of what is called birth. Thus, man came to be an entity, a human being. Man cannot know precisely how this came about; we only know that it did. Man cannot know when it came about or by what specific process. We only know that it did. But if our intelligence is correct, this beginning occurred hundreds of thousands, perhaps millions of years ago by man's method of marking time.

All things that God created are infused with spirit. It is the sustaining force contained within all things, both animate and inanimate. And though a thing may appear to be non-living, it nonetheless is sustained by the spirit of God. Only God is able to provide the spirit that gives substance to all things.

God gave man an intricate body to house an even more intricate mind, and working together, the mind and body keep one another alive and functioning. With his unique mind came the ability to create, that is, to change the world around him. And further, God gave man the freedom to do so. Additionally, God instilled his own essence into man, and it seems into man alone. It seems that man alone houses within himself the God essence, that is, the knowledge of the infinite nature of all in existence. The seat of this unique characteristic in man he has come to call his soul. The intangible soul is the true self of the tangible man. The soul is man's immortality.

So the soul is the essence of God residing within man. The body is merely the vehicle in which the soul dwells, somewhere near the heart in its own special place. The brain enables the soul to communicate and instruct. We can surely sense the presence of the soul, just as we can feel the beating of the heart. It is the duty of the soul to act as man's conscience. It is also the duty of the soul to keep man on a godly path in life. It is the soul that enables man to recognize and understand the meaning of his own being. Once a man learns to communicate with his own soul rather than rely on the thoughts and words of others, he will begin to appreciate the reason for his being.

If you believe in God, then you can easily believe in the human soul. As already stated, the human soul is the equivalent of God within us, the image of God as it were. It is therefore as the Bible informs us, man is made in the image of God. We may not understand what this means or choose to accept it, but we are all made in God's image. This is not to demean God or to exalt man. It is just the way it is by God's own design.

Although the soul will be discussed later, I would like to make a preemptive comment and that is that the soul of man is eternal. Unlike the mind and body, which are inseparable and dependent upon the breath of life, the soul functions not independent of but rather superior to the physical aspects of man. In fact, the soul plays an intricate and deliberate part in a man's life and has choices regarding the birth, life, and death of the physical entity. The soul continues to thrive after physical death. Individual soul natures of mankind have emanated from the unified collection of all souls known as the universal soul. The universal soul is immortal, eternal, and will be discussed later.

With regard to natural progression, I may be wrong. I forget that there are many who do not believe in God. This does not mean that they are not responsible for their own spiritual enlightenment. Non-believers are as much

God's creation as any other man or woman. They, too, are made in God's image and are inheritors of God's plan for mankind. It could be that an acceptance of the human soul, of its responsibility to man, of reincarnation and of karma might just open a non-believer's mind and heart to the reality of the existence of God. But when all is said and done, it is behind closed doors and within private sanctuaries that man and God commune. It is only within the uttermost privacy of *self* that truth is made known to man according to his own need, and in his own time, and in his own tongue, and in accordance with the will of God.

GOD, PART ONE

A sunbeam, a sunbeam, Jesus wants me for a sunbeam.
A sunbeam, a sunbeam, I'll be a sunbeam for him.

I remember it as though it was yesterday. This little musical mantra at the age of three was the beginning of my religious education in a very large Southern Baptist church in the capitol city of the state in which I was born and now live. From beginners, we graduated through the age progressive stages of primary, junior, and intermediate. By this time, we were well versed in the popular biblical stories, the various heroes and villains, the good and bad aspects of man, and most of us had been baptized. We could quote dozens of Bible verses from memory, name the books of the Bible by rote, sing most of the songs in the Broadman Hymnal without looking at the words, and we had done our share of visiting the homebound and ministering to the needy.

We knew we were sinners and constantly prayed for forgiveness as well as for all sinners of the world. We routinely uttered prayers of both petition and thanks. We knew beyond all doubt that our salvation had been bought and paid for by Jesus Christ, and no one could take that away from us as long as we believed in him—*John* 3:16-17. We were safe for all time. We had reached that pinnacle necessary for avoiding Hell and attaining eternal life. And yet, at that tender age, none of us had experienced enough of life to put all that learning and doing into perspective or to be really appreciative of what we had gained or believed we had gained. That education was to come soon enough.

As we began the stage of young adulthood, things began to happen, things that didn't jibe with the rosy outlook on life that we had been given. There is no need to go into detail. All have experienced the growing pains, figuratively as well as literally, that come with aging. People we thought were bad were not so bad after all. People we thought were good were not so good after all, and both were fewer in number than we had earlier thought. We learned that most of us function somewhere in between good and bad, between making right and wrong choices.

But perhaps the rudest awakening for me was the realization that, theology-wise, I did not like some of the things that I was being expected to believe, even required to believe if indeed I was to be "saved." Primarily, I didn't like the idea of Hell. I just couldn't, wouldn't believe that God, my all-loving, all-forgiving Creator, would ordain such an atrocity as Hell. This became very troubling for me, especially because someone very dear to me told me that if I didn't believe in Hell then I was not a true Christian. These words, coming from a loved one, crushed my spirit and cut into my heart. It instilled in my mind a self-doubt that took me many, many years to resolve.

Coming on the heels of this deflating experience was the guilt I felt due to the fact that I began to think that Jesus was not as perfect as the church teaches he was. I think that Jesus was not perfect. Jesus showed a lack of respect for his parents at the age of twelve. Jesus had a temper tantrum in the temple. Although he was Mary's first born, Jesus largely ignored her, leaving it up to others to see to her well-being. Jesus exhibited a lack of patience with his dedicated disciples and followers when they were slow to understand his words and teachings. In all humility, these negatives were things that I myself had largely been able to rise above—me, a mere mortal. But most importantly, Jesus did not really want to die for the sake of or the sins of others. He pleaded with God to allow him to live. Was that a breach of faith? He did so twice on the night he was arrested and tried by the Jewish religious establishment before being given over to the Romans for crucifixion. As he died, he lamented, "Father, why have you forsaken me?" Was that a breach of faith?

Several times, I have attempted to read the Bible through and through, but, you know, I cannot get past the first few books of the Old Testament. The Old Testament records immoralities and atrocities among 'god's people,' the 'chosen race,' that rival the most decadent of horror stories on the screen today. And in the middle of all of that—and even initiating much of it—was the Hebrew 'god,' Jehovah. Jehovah **is** the god of the Old Testament. That **is** his name. He gave it to Moses and insisted it be used. But try as I might, I cannot pray to Jehovah. Can you?

Over the years, I have come to learn significant facts about the Bible such as the gospels were not necessarily written by the disciple that each is named for but were mostly written by other authors and were actually written much, much later than the occurrences they relate. Further, the gospels do not agree with one another on certain really important details. For one, there are errors regarding Jesus's genealogy. Two different genealogies are cited with each being purported to be the lineage through Joseph. But consider this: Joseph was not the biological father, so, unless one of the genealogies is Mary's, neither is valid in tracing Jesus's link to the House of David, which was prophesied that he would be.

Jesus has his counterpart in many other and older religions. Many biblical events are told in other and much older cultures including the account in *The Revelation of St. John*. And so on and so forth. It becomes clear that the Bible is not written in the words of God but in the words of men. The Bible therefore is not a holy book; it is simply an inspirational book as well as being the account of the appearance and early history of a single race of man—Adam's descendants, the Israelites. If the Bible is a holy book—the word of God—there would not be so many versions of it. There are a number of versions, and the widely used and accepted King James Version is a latecomer. Now there is the NKJV, the *New King James Version*.

With all this negativity being expressed, you may well wonder how on Earth my religious training has contributed to my spiritual understanding. The truth is that it has contributed very little. What has put me onto the path and kept me on a steady course with regard to spiritual understanding is my profound belief in God as I was originally taught. For this, I can thank my parents. You see, our Creator is an all-pervading, all-powerful God who loves all equally and forgives anything and everything. But the church has twisted that ideology and changed it into a reward/punishment, Heaven or

Hell, choose-right-or-die-horribly doctrine. Worse, it has attributed human characteristics and qualities to God. The church has created a manmade God, which they believe belongs exclusively to a certain few. Paul admonished the Romans:

> Romans 1:22-23
> *"Professing themselves to be wise, they became fools, and changed the glory of the uncorruptible God into an image made like to corruptible man."*

Let's look at a conventional definition of God. *God: the supreme or ultimate reality—the Being perfect in power, wisdom and goodness who men worship as Creator and ruler of the universe—the incorporeal Divine Principle ruling over all as Eternal Spirit: Infinite Mind.* This is not an adequate or even remotely conclusive definition of God, but it will suffice for now.

The first thing to understand is that there is but one God. No one has ever seen God. No one has ever walked with God. God has never spoken to any man. We refer to God as *He* strictly for the sake of convenience in making reference to God. No one knows what God looks like, if He indeed does look like anything at all. God has been described as spirit, power, mind. I think of God as essence. Look in any dictionary, and you will find that the word essence has varied meanings, all somewhat ethereal. God is an intangible essence that cannot be touched, yet He is sensed intuitively by the human mind and soul. Man, in his mind "knows" and in his soul knows and accepts that there is something beyond infinity that represents the seed or the beginning of all that exists. God is that essence, that seed, that starting point.

The essence that is God is omniscient, all knowing. The essence that is God is omnipotent, all powerful. The essence that is God is omnipresent, everywhere. God has infused His very spirit into everything that exists in the physical world to which we belong. Without the spirit of God nothing would exist, nothing physical or otherwise. God has infused His very essence into man. In this respect, man *is* made in the image of God. The essence of God in man is generally referred to as soul or the soul.

Most of the world's religions believe that their God, by whatever name they call him, is the one true God and that all other religions must be worshiping the wrong god. In fact, all religions that worship one god are actually worshipping the same god that is the essence that is responsible for forming the universe and all that exists within it. They are worshiping an omnipotent, omniscient, omnipresent god. And we know that there is but one who fits the bill.

Some may see God in the sun or in an animal or in a geological formation, *etc*. This is of no real consequence because it is the God essence that is worshipped. A real and divisive problem arises when one sect believes that the god of another sect cannot be the one and only god; this problem arises primarily due to differences in practices and expectations. The problem is compounded when man insists on conferring human qualities and emotions and motivations to their god such as happiness, sadness, regret, remorse, anger, revenge, ego, pride, etc. Once this happens, that religion is no longer worshiping God. They have created a manmade, man-like god. And I believe, unfortunately, this is the situation with most religions worldwide. Most religious sects with their pomp and circumstance, their practices, rites and rituals, their testimonies and sacrifices, their self-righteous and hypocritical attitudes, their secretive and not so secretive lustful desires are not on a spiritual path, they are on a worldly path. They neither perceive God as God is nor do they understand man and God's true relationship.

I have had a very deep concern for a long time now that the church—the Christian church—has lost sight of just who and what it is about. Christianity was begun by the followers of the man Jesus who they considered to be the Messiah, the Savior, or Christ. The religious movement was given the name in honor of Jesus, the Christ, or Jesus Christ. In my mind, Christianity is about God. God is the foundation of my belief system. He and He alone is the focal point. But I have observed a shifting of focus from God to the man Jesus. Rather than maintain faith in our unseen Creator, today's Christianity is more and more beginning to focus on the more tangible, historical Jesus. I seldom hear anyone pray to God these days. Everyone seems to pray to Jesus. Rather than thank God for their blessings, they thank Jesus. Rather than ask

God for their needs, they ask Jesus. Rather than ask God for healing, they ask Jesus. I find it hard to express how difficult this is for me to accept. It seems to me that today's Christians have elevated the person of Jesus and relegated God to the background. And I believe that this practice has lent great weight to the charge that "God is dead." But God is not dead. God is very much alive and in control.

If you have read *Genesis: A Tale Twice Told*, then you know that in my mind the conventional Hell and its equivalent that so many religions allude to does not exist. And you also know that it is my profound belief that Jesus was a man, not God come to Earth. The notion of Hell sprang from paganism. The idea that Jesus is God springs from the doctrine of the Trinity, three gods in one. One has only to scratch the surface of religious history or research into the Trinity to know that this doctrine, too, came down directly from paganism. Numerous religions much, much older than Christianity are based on a triad of deities. The three-in-one theme is ancient and pagan in origin. This being said, I return to my premise that Christianity is putting God on the back burner in favor of the more visible, easier to accept, Jesus. But I have an even more egregious grievance against today's Christian church. In *Genesis: A Tale Twice Told*, I charged Christianity with worshipping a false god. And I do so here, as well.

GOD, PART TWO

*In the beginning, God created the heavens and the earth . . .
Jehovah planted a garden in Eden, toward the East,
and there he put the man whom he had formed.*

When I began my project to find out just when Adam appeared on Earth, I was determined that the answer must come from the Bible. That would be the only source that I would accept. I did however decide to also utilize the Jehovah Witness Bible, thinking that it may have been translated more accurately from the original languages that the scriptures were written in than the *King James Version* had. I thought of it as a validation if the two versions agreed. I found that the two versions did agree on the numerical data, even though the wording was slightly different here and there.

As I continued to work back and forth between the two books, I began to notice a consistent difference in one respect. Beginning in Genesis 2, everywhere the *King James Version* had the terms Lord and Lord God, the *New World Translation* had the terms Jehovah and Jehovah God. And in subsequent chapters, the *New World Translation* began to make the distinction 'the [true] god.' I thought to myself: *What is going on here?*

As I continued delving into the unfolding events around the descendants of Adam, it became painfully clear that the god in the books of *Genesis* and *Exodus*, in fact, in all the Old Testament, was not at all godly. It hit me like the proverbial ton of bricks. The entity that placed Adam and Eve in the garden in Eden was not God but an interloper posing as God the Creator.

I immediately thought of the story that most of us have heard about the archangel Lucifer being cast out of Heaven for desiring to become an equal or co-creator with God. He was given temporary control or power over the earth, and he became known as Satan. His desire was to become accepted as God himself. Did Satan set about the task of 'creating' Adam patterned after the mankind already roaming the earth at that time? Did Satan go about the task of deceiving mankind by posing as God and by performing actions that man did not understand and would consider "miracles"? Is Satan the entity who walked and talked with Abraham? Is Satan the entity who, over twenty-six hundred years after "creating" Adam, finally divulged his real identity to Moses? It boggles the mind to think of this possibility.

I believe that most "believers" think of the Lucifer scenario as myth. I know I always have. We talk about Satan being here on Earth, but don't most of us think of this as being allegorical narrative? I always have.

Without a doubt, evil not only exists but runs rampant over the face of the earth. But evil is a condition, not an entity. It is man who has given substance and an identity to evil. And it is man who can disenfranchise Satan and overcome evil simply by saying, "No." I do not believe that the entity Jehovah was Satan, though he did embody the spirit of evil that is represented by the perception of Satan. One need not fear Satan. Satan has no real power over the human soul. However, evil does. Evil must be recognized and neutralized. This is the innate duty and goal of the human soul, both individually and collectively.

No, Jehovah is not Satan. I have another even more mind-boggling explanation as to who Jehovah was or is. Being a logic-oriented thinker, I need an explanation that does not smack of myth but one that has reasonable probability of being true, based on tangible evidence; where tangible evidence does not exist then at least there are clues that point to genuine possibility.

There is, of course, no undeniable proof concerning Jehovah that I know of. But there are many clues that have led me to the conclusion that I will express here. So as not to keep you hanging, let me state that I believe that Jehovah was/is an entity not only from beyond our own solar system but probably from beyond our own galaxy. And I am not referring to a fallen angel but to what is commonly referred to as an alien being.

The earth with its trillions of life forms is but a speck in the totality of all that exists. This is an obvious fact. Most people today are willing to accept the genuine probability that there is life in deep outer space. Additionally, most people are willing to accept at least the possibility that "beings" or some form of intelligent life from outer space has indeed visited our earth and left their mark not only by way of innovation but in actual physical expression such as the drawings and lines on the plains of Nazca in Peru. And there is much more.

Many books have been written about the probability that aliens have visited the earth. My favorite author on the subject of alien visitation is Erich von Daniken. His writings are based on research and on actual visual evidence and other reasonable clues. The first book I read by von Daniken was *Chariots of the Gods?* It made a lot of sense to me. There is also *The Outer Space Connection*, a very informative and believable documentary. But just as I was insistent that the six-thousand-year question be answered in the Bible, I am just as insistent that the probability of alien visitation must be indicated in the Bible if it is to answer certain questions surrounding Adam, Jehovah, 'miracles,' etc.

Even though I had read the *Genesis* account many times, it was not until I began researching it that certain details stood out that had previously escaped my attention. Specifically, I began to notice the proximity of God to the garden in Eden.

> Genesis 3:8, NWT
> *"Later they heard the voice of Jehovah God walking in the garden about the breezy part of the day, and the man and his wife went into hiding from the face of Jehovah God in between the trees of the garden."*

What? Does that say that God was *walking* in the garden? Adam and Eve heard the *voice* of God and hid from the *face* of God? God was actually **in** the garden? The implication of those words had never really sunk in before. I had been taught that God has never been on Earth. This accounting flew in the face of that contention.

As a young Christian, I had always wondered why God placed the trees in the garden if he did not want Adam and Eve to partake of the fruit of the trees of life and of knowledge. Even more puzzling, why did he plant the trees in the center of the garden where they could not be missed, where they were a constant temptation? God is omniscient as well as all-loving. It seems somewhat ambivalent and certainly unnecessary that God would need to test Adam and Eve's loyalty or obedience to him. I also wondered why God would not want Adam and Eve to gain knowledge or an understanding of life. The serpent explained regarding knowledge: Jehovah did not want Adam and Eve to partake of the fruit of the tree of knowledge because in doing so they would become like *the gods*. They would gain the ability to discern between good and evil. Jehovah did not want his beings to have this ability. But Adam and Eve both helped themselves to this forbidden fruit.

Jehovah himself answered the question regarding the tree of life. Why did he not want Adam and Eve to partake of the fruit of the tree of life?

> Genesis 3:22-23 NWT
> *"And Jehovah God went on to say: 'Here the man has become like one of us in knowing good and bad, and now in order that he may not put his hand out and actually take fruit also of the tree of life and eat and live to time indefinite' – With that Jehovah put him out of the garden of Eden to cultivate the ground from which he had been taken."*

Jehovah did not want Adam and Eve to learn the secret of eternal life. But isn't eternal life the goal of every Christian and the ultimate gift of God? I believe it to be the ever-present reality for all unless it is lost through the downward spiraling of soul regression. I understand that some souls will choose to wallow in ungodliness and refuse to adhere to or return to the innocence of their birth. It is possible that some souls will relinquish their connection to the universal soul and ignore the desire and the quest for world peace, for love between and among all men. It is possible that some souls will perish into oblivion, into a state of nothingness and cease to be. I have not achieved a level of discernment pertaining to what will happen to those souls who *refuse* the gift of everlasting life. What do you think?

Jehovah was determined that Adam and Eve would not learn the secret of eternal life, so

> "...*he drove the man out and posted at the east of the garden of Eden the cherubs and the flaming blade of a sword that was turning itself continually to guard the way to the tree of life.*"

As readers, we really do skirt over small details, don't we, especially if they pertain to a hard-to-explain situation. Just what visual does this verse provide? Do you see angels and an orbiting, flaming sword? I see guards and a rotating searchlight. The use of a searchlight would involve a very advanced knowledge for that time period. To me, it suggests the workings of a very advanced intelligence and a clue to the possibility of intervention by an entity alien to Earth. And isn't it odd that the serpent referred to *gods* in the plural? And isn't it odd that Jehovah stated, "Here the man has become like *one of us*"? To me, this statement alone belies Jehovah being God.

Going back to the formation of Eve from a rib taken from Adam, today we have cloning and test tube babies, so this was not as miraculous as it sounds. The next clue definitely suggesting alien involvement came as I began to record the actual genealogy of Adam and his descendants. From Adam and progressing through six generations, there was a consistent pattern in the account. Each patriarch was named and his age given followed by the words, "and he died."

But then came the naming of the seventh generation patriarch, Enoch. We are given the age of Enoch but not the words, "and he died."

> Genesis 5:23-24, KJV
> "*And all the days of Enoch were three hundred, sixty and five years: And Enoch walked with God: and he was not; for God took him.*"

Just to be sure I was not overreacting to this anomaly, I checked the *New World Translation* to see what it said. Here, the same chapter and verses as noted above read:

> "So all the days of Enoch amounted to three hundred and sixty-five years. And Enoch kept walking with the [true] God. Then he was no more, for God took him."

What in the world does this mean? Clearly it suggests that Enoch did not experience a physical death as his forebears had and as well as we are all subject to. Fast forward to our current place in time, and keeping in mind the suggestion of a searchlight in Eden, how would the event of Enoch being "taken" be interpreted today? Alien abduction has a sinister connotation, so let's just say, a close encounter of the fourth kind.

Before we leave the subject of the progression of Adam and those who came after him, I feel it pertinent to mention their life spans: Adam lived 930 years, Methuselah lived 969 years, Noah lived 950 years, Abraham lived 175 years, and Jacob (Israel) lived 147 years. Does Christian theology even question, much less attempt to explain, these life spans? I have never heard it discussed except to have it said that God's years must not be the same as man's years.

Like von Daniken, I believe it was due to the fact that Adam and Eve were hybrids. I believe that their genetic makeup was the combination of earthly man and the genes of whatever life form Jehovah represents. Further, I believe that their incubation took place in a laboratory of some sophistication. I believe that their 'birth' was achieved by some sort of artificial contrived process. I believe that their intelligence was the product of a kind of fast lane or even instantaneous learning process. I also have considered that, since they came into being in this fashion that they did not possess souls, they were not the image of God. The soul enters the body during or shortly before or after birth. When did Adam and Eve receive their souls if they did? Was this the nakedness of Adam and Eve? Was knowledge of this fact the forbidden fruit?

Hybridization: The combination of the genes of two different species of organisms with the resulting organism being a new and unique life form.

Without question, the Bible describes hybridization having occurred. It also suggests that the days of the hybrids would be numbered since Jehovah and his kind would not remain on Earth indefinitely.

> Genesis 6:1-4 NWT
> *"Now it came about that when men started to grow in numbers on the surface of the ground and daughters were born to them, then the sons of the [true] God began to notice the daughters of men, that they were good looking; and they went taking wives for themselves, namely, all whom they chose. After that Jehovah said: 'My spirit shall not act toward man indefinitely in that he is also flesh. Accordingly his days shall amount to a hundred and twenty years.' The Nephilim proved to be in the earth in those days, and also after that, when, the sons of the [true] God continued to have relations with the daughters of men and they bore sons to them, they were the mighty ones who were of old, the men of fame."* (The KJV uses the term "giants" for the word Nephilim.)

Now in my mind, this is the explanation for the extended life spans of Adam and his descendants. It also explains that this propensity for long life was slowly out-bred in that Jehovah and his kind did not remain on Earth, so that the human gene became dominant. No one knows the days/years formula utilized in the early biblical prophecies, but you can be sure that the numbers were precise, accurate, and significant with regard to hidden meanings and future events.

There are many clues suggestive of alien intervention and demigods contained within the Bible, but I am mentioning only those that stood out to me as I studied the books of *Genesis* and *Exodus*. The strongest and most obvious clues come from the account of Moses and the exodus of the Israelites from Egypt. Why some people cannot see these clues is beyond me. They are so clearly obvious.

Let's start with the "call." Much ado has been made about the manner in which God called Moses into service—the miraculous occurrence of the burning bush. Native to the area is a plant called Dittany that emits an oily substance that coats the leaves. This substance is so volatile that the heat from the sun can cause the oil to ignite. When this happens, the plant appears to be on fire, but it is simply the oil being burned away. The plant is not harmed at all. Aside from several scientific names for the different varieties of this plant, it is familiarly called gas plant or burning bush. So much for that miracle!

Jehovah had called on Moses and his brother Aaron to rescue the Israelites from their bondage in Egypt. Since the time of Abraham, the Israelites had been known as "the people of one god." Moses and Aaron were sent into Egypt to get permission for the Israelites to leave Egypt and go into the wilderness supposedly to celebrate a festival to their god. The name of their god, Jehovah, had not been told to them. The Israelites had literally been the slave force in Egypt for over four hundred years. Jehovah had told Moses that Egypt's pharaoh would not be agreeable to their leaving Egypt, so he instructed Moses and Aaron on how to perform certain illusions, which would be perceived as miracles and convince the pharaoh that the Israelite's god was more powerful than his own. I use the term "illusions" because, at first, the pharaoh's magicians could produce the same "miracles," or illusions that Moses was performing.

There are many really talented illusionists who perform unbelievable feats of "magic" these days. But we all know that these feats are really just tricks, illusions. It seems that many of Moses's so-called miracles can be understood in light of today's scientific knowledge and the skill of modern-day illusionists. When illusions failed to impress the pharaoh, Jehovah brought about ten plagues on the land of Egypt. Oddly enough, Jehovah had told Moses in advance that he would harden the pharaoh's heart following each plague so that he would not let the people go. Right away we have to suspect that Jehovah is up to something.

The first plague was turning the waters of the Nile River into blood. We are put in mind of "red tides," whole bodies of water that appear to be red due to the growth of a certain algae on the surface. This condition occurred in Vancouver in July of 2014. It can be a natural condition or it can be brought on by the introduction of certain chemicals or toxins into the water. Either or both possibilities could have been the situation in Egypt. We are told that the pharaoh's magicians were able to duplicate this action, the turning of the water into blood.

Then there was the plague of frogs. When the Nile became toxic due to a red tide, millions of frogs came up out of the water and covered the land. With nothing to eat, the frogs died. Additionally, the fish in the river died and washed ashore. There followed the plague of gnats, which naturally appeared on the dead and rotting frogs as well as on the millions of beached dead fish and other water-borne organisms.

Next came biting flies, also drawn to the rotting frogs and fish. One plague led to another. The gnats and flies carried disease to animals and humans, death to the animals and boils to the humans.

Then there was a rain of hail that beat down the crops. I understand that man is now capable of producing certain weather patterns by the use of cloud seeding and, more recently, directed energy. Following the hail were the locusts, which totally consumed the remaining crops. This event may have been foreknown. We are reminded of the Cicada locust, which lives underground but predictably surfaces every seventeen years to reproduce, only to return below ground to remain for seventeen years before repeating this routine event.

These plagues were followed by three days of darkness. The sun did not shine through at all. This was most likely due to a severe dust storm. Dust storms are common in the area.

I have read various possible and probable scientific explanations for all the plagues, even the final one—the death of every first born, both human and beast. Whereas the first nine plagues are easily explained, this final one has not been explained to my satisfaction. I believe it was carried out by Jehovah's agents. In our lifetime, we have witnessed corrupt governments commit chemical genocide in order to eliminate specific targeted factions of a population in large numbers.

We need to keep in mind that the Israelites did not reside in the main cities of Egypt, especially not where the pharaoh and other royals lived. They lived a considerable distance away in an area called Goshen, much as religious sects today live in "no go" sections of large cities and countries. They kept to themselves. To avoid being included in the final plague, the Israelites had been instructed by Moses to kill sacrificial lambs and place marks using lambs' blood over the entrances to their homes. That night, the Angel of Death passed through the land, and the first born of every household that did not bear the mark of the lambs' blood died. That night, the first born of every Egyptian household died as well as the first born of every beast. This was the straw that broke the pharaoh's back. He demanded Moses to take all the Israelites and leave Egypt.

As mentioned earlier, it was Jehovah's plan to purposely harden the pharaoh's heart after each plague so that he would not let the Israelites go. Jehovah himself had told Moses ahead of time what he planned to do. If Jehovah really wanted his people rescued from enslavement, then why did he keep causing the Pharaoh to refuse?

> Exodus 9:14, 16 NWT (Jehovah to Pharaoh)
> *"For at this time I am sending all my blows against your heart and upon your servants and your people, to the end that you may know that there is none like me in all the earth."*
>
> *"But, in fact, for this cause I have kept you in existence, for the sake of showing you my power and in order to have my name declared in all the earth."*

If Jehovah was truly empathetic to the suffering of his people in Egypt, why didn't he just produce a miracle and take his people out, preferably directly to the land of milk and honey that he had promised to Abraham? Why was it necessary for him to cause the extensive suffering, destruction, and death that preceded the exodus? Does this sound like something God would do? (I am curious about the phrase "in all the earth.") Shortly after allowing the Israelites to leave Egypt, the pharaoh had a change of heart. He saw that there was no festival in the desert but that, in fact, his slave force was escaping. He sent his armies in pursuit to capture and return the Israelites to Egypt.

We have got to keep in mind what the exodus entailed. There were six hundred thousand able-bodied men (*Exodus* 12:37-38) as well as mothers, daughters, wives, the elderly—both male and female—and many children of both sexes together with their household and personal belongings, tools, tents, equipment, herds of cattle, sheep, goats, fowl, etc. This was no camp meeting they were undertaking. Moses was leading over two million Israelites, but who was leading Moses? We know it was Jehovah, but where was he taking them and just how did he go about it?

>Exodus 13: 21-22
>*"And Jehovah was going ahead of them in the daytime in a pillar of cloud to lead them by the way, and in the nighttime in a pillar of fire to give them light to go in the daytime, and nighttime. The pillar of cloud would not move away from before the people in the daytime nor the pillar of fire in the nighttime."*

So they were moving day and night. With such a large assembly, they must have moved in shifts. Some would rest while others traveled, led by a cloud by day and a light by night.

This was no ordinary cloud such as you and I are accustomed to seeing. This cloud did not shift in shape or density. It had a very specific shape. It formed a pillar or a column that retained its shape. It was fixed in its shape and in its position. It did not move away from before the Israelites. However, it did move. It moved of its own free will and in any direction it wanted. It was leading the Israelites out of and away from the land of Egypt, supposedly to the Promised Land. No, this cloud did not rely on the winds to carry it along. The when and where of its movement was self-determined. In other words, the cloud either had intelligence or there was some form of intelligence concealed within the cloud. Which makes more sense?

Not only did the cloud lead them by day but it provided light for the Israelites during the night. At night, a pillar of fire emanated from the cloud. Have you and I witnessed "pillars of fire" emanating from hovering or overhead objects? Could this pillar of fire have been a beam of light such as a running light or a searchlight? Later, when the Egyptians pursued the Israelites, at night the cloud moved from in front of the encampment to its rear, positioning itself between the Israelites and the approaching Egyptian soldiers. All through the night, it cast down beams of light in front of itself in order to facilitate the continuing movement of the Israelites, but the light was not visible from behind the pillar of light. From the Egyptians vantage point, there was only darkness, which served to halt their progress and hold them at bay, giving the Israelites the advantage.

Just as a matter of interest, did you know that this same cloud or one like it as well as the pillar of fire appears in the Mormon epic, which is more or less a small-scale parallel version of the escape from Egypt a thousand years after Moses, around six hundred years before Jesus? The Mormon epic incorporated a number of Old Testament characters and events. The Mormon account begins during the first year of the reign of King Zedekiah, king of the Israelis' southern kingdom of Judah. It involves the destruction of the city of Jerusalem and the temple by Babylon's King Nebuchadnezzar; the wilderness surrounding the Red Sea; a Jew named Lehi, his wife, Sariah, and their family; and dissension, brother against brother, murder, etc. Mormonism recognizes the name Jehovah. And it was their god, the Lord (Jehovah) who commanded one brother to slay another. Nothing seems to ever get better with Adam's god. Hardship, death, and destruction—the order of the day, and on and on it goes.

Back to Moses and his undertaking. As stated, the Israelites lived in an area of Egypt called Goshen (see *Exodus* 8:22 and *Exodus* 9:26). You can find a good map of the exodus route on the Internet. Goshen is near the northern Mediterranean Sea border of Egypt. So which route out of Egypt did Jehovah choose? Remember that the goal was to reach the Promised Land, which we assume was located somewhere to the east to what is today the northern border of Syria or Iraq since that is where the exodus eventually ended and the occupation began with the destruction of the city of Jericho. You would expect the Israelites to be taken on as directly east a route as possible. It would have been a relatively short trip compared to the actual route that was taken. For starters, Jehovah led Moses southward into a dead end at the southern tip of what is today Israel. The only way out was to turn around and back track, but they could not do that. Pharaoh's armies were in pursuit. So it was time for another "miracle." You have to wonder if this was not the plan all along.

Jehovah had already told Moses that he had brought the plagues on Egypt as a means of showing his power. So he does it again. By means of a strong east wind, he caused a land bridge to appear across the narrow Red Sea from bank to bank, allowing the entire body of Israelites to cross over the sea bed to the opposite bank. This had to have been a very strong and sustained wind to allow the enormous body of Israelites to get across the sea. Egypt's army came right behind them, but as the last Israelite made it safely across, Jehovah allowed the waters to fall back and swallow up every last Egyptian.

I have seen a number of explanations of how the parting of the waters of the Red Sea could have been accomplished. Some rely on natural phenomena and others on manual manipulation. All are very plausible, and each is believable and possible. I personally choose to believe that the "east wind" that parted the water was the wind from a very large rapidly rotating overhead object, an air ship of some kind that moved ahead of the Israelites. This airborne object was concealed within the cloud. It accounts for the intelligence within the cloud mentioned earlier. Because of a lack of knowledge, understanding, and acceptance, this object today would be classified as a UFO. In the days of Moses, there was no explanation for it other than it being god performing a miracle.

So now that the Israelites are across the Red Sea, you might think that their journey was nearing its end. Well, it was only beginning. Keep in mind that they had already traveled nearly three hundred miles in the wrong direction. Now they must head back north. But now that they are basically free of natural obstructions and the Egyptians, it should be easy sailing, right? Not right! We all know that the shortest distance between two points is a straight line. Like I said, do your reference work and locate a map of the wilderness journey of the freed Israelites. You will be shocked at the roundabout zigzagging and doubling back. (Try www. bible.ca/exodus)

Jehovah led the Israelites around and about the desert for forty years before taking them to the Promised Land, which is what Jehovah had promised to Abraham for his descendants seven hundred years earlier. It would be a land flowing with milk and honey. During the forty years of wandering in the wilderness, Jehovah gave Moses the Ten Commandments and a plethora of rules to be followed and rituals to be observed.

The entire encampment dismantled and moved forty times, once each year. The Israelites began to doubt Jehovah. There was much frustration, unrest and in-fighting. Moses's brother, Aaron, fashioned a calf made of gold, and the Israelites began to worship it. There was much bloodshed as brother killed brother. Additionally, as the Israelites traveled through populated areas, they went as an army, murdering the inhabitants and completely destroying the cities. They gained a reputation for being a mighty and bloodthirsty force, and were greatly feared. Jehovah had promised this and proudly took the credit for it.

The Promised Land was not a beautiful, serene landscape just waiting to be occupied. It was already occupied by various Canaanite or Arabic tribes that would have to be fought and destroyed. The occupation of the lands of others by Israel reached a temporary climax with the destruction of the city of Jericho. I don't know that the actual location of ancient Jericho is known, but the Israelites did have to cross the Jordan River to get to it. It was a crossing much like the parting of the Red Sea. The destruction of Jericho was complete. Its inhabitants, along with every beast were slain, and the city was burned to the ground. With Jehovah's aid and blessing, this is how Israel got its homeland, the Promised Land thirty-five-hundred years ago. They killed for it. They stole it.

It just occurred to me, and I will remind the reader, that the Israelites would have had a homeland had Jehovah not twice torn them from their origins. He drove Adam out of Eden and then later destroyed almost all of Adam's descendants and the land they were occupying with the great flood. From that point on, with the exception of scattered pockets of homesteaders, the chosen lineage was nomadic, strangers in every territory they wandered into. Jehovah dealt the race another blow when they attempted to put down roots, by scattering them at the site of the tower of Babel.

At this juncture, I would like to point out what probably few Christians know and that is that not one of the Israelites who walked out of Egypt lived to see the Promise Land. Not one. Not even Moses. He died by the order of Jehovah, whatever that means.

> Deuteronomy 34:4-7
> *"Moses the servant of Jehovah died there . . . at the order of Jehovah ... And Moses was a hundred and twenty years old at his death. His eye had not grown dim, and his vital strength had not fled."*

You would think that, like Enoch, Jehovah would have taken Moses unto himself after the service he had performed. But Moses had inadvertently disobeyed Jehovah once with regard to striking a rock to find water. He didn't follow Jehovah's instructions exactly. For this act of independence, Jehovah did not allow Moses to enter the Promised Land. This is perhaps one of my greatest grievances against the injustice of Jehovah and his ways.

Jehovah is no god. By his own words, *"Jehovah is a man of war."* He is nothing more than an egoistic demi-god, a want-to-be. That the Christian and the Jewish churches worship him as God is a human tragedy. It has kept mankind from realizing and understanding his spiritual nature and his connection with God the Creator. This is what Jesus tried his best to teach mankind. Jesus **is** a savior for those who listen to and believe his words:

> John 5:24, NWT
> *"Most truly I say to you, He that hears my word and believes him that sent me has everlasting life, and he does not come into judgment but has passed over from death to life."*

The Old Testaments of the Christian and the Jewish bibles are crampacked with evidence that Jehovah is not God. The Old Testament saga is also replete with clues that Jehovah did not originate here on Earth. It is easy to understand how Jehovah, with his advanced skills and knowledge, fooled early man in the past. But despite his skills and knowledge, he is undeniably prideful, fallible, and vengeful, characteristics that cannot be attributed to God. In light of this, it is difficult to understand why Christianity and Judaism cannot see through the ruse.

In this section, we have considered who and what God is not. God is not Jehovah. Jehovah is not God. Before moving ahead, I want to list various points noted in the books of *Genesis* and *Exodus* that to me represent clues that Jehovah is not God and is in fact a being from outside the realm of the earth. Please keep in mind that the *Genesis/Exodus* saga took place just six thousand years ago. This is a fact gleaned from these very books of the Bible themselves. Some of the following clues I have already mentioned and some I have not. Unless otherwise noted, I am using the *New World Translation* because I believe it translates the original scriptures more accurately.

> Genesis 2:4-8
> *Now there was as yet no bush of the field found in the earth and no vegetation of the field was as yet sprouting, because Jehovah God had not made it rain upon the earth and there was no man to cultivate the ground. And Jehovah God proceeded to form the man out of dust from the ground…*

In a barren area, Jehovah formed a man, utilizing earth materials, the basic elements that make up the human body, i.e., hydrogen, oxygen, proteins, inorganic salts, *etc*. No vegetation was present in that place at that time. After engendering Adam, Jehovah planted a garden to house him. Logically, and if we are to believe the first chapter of *Genesis*, plant life preceded man not the other way around. And Adam, having come into being a mere six thousand years ago, was not the first man on Earth. This was not the creation but a subsequent action taken by a knowledgeable entity of unknown origin.

Also, there were many men tilling the earth. Cultivation had become an established way of life in the ancient East three thousand years earlier. This is a historical fact.

> Genesis 2:19
> *"Now Jehovah God was forming from the ground every wild beast of the field and every flying creature of the heavens, and he began bringing them to the man to see what he would call each one."*

Again, if Chapter 1 of *Genesis* is to be considered, following plant life, fish and fowl appeared on Earth and only after that the beasts of the field. Fish, fowl, and beasts preceded Adam, not the other way around. This is a natural progression, nature's way. After forming Adam and then planting a garden to house him, Jehovah formed animals and birds (from the materials of the earth) and took them to Adam for companionship and for Adam to give names to. This collection of animal life was of Jehovah's doing by whatever means he had at his disposal or by whatever process he had knowledge of.

None of the animals were compatible with Adam's chemistry; therefore none was suitable as a mate for him. Just a small oversight, I suppose.

> Genesis 2:22-23
> *"And Jehovah God proceeded to build the rib that he had taken from the man into a woman and to bring her to the man. Then the man said: "This is at last bone of my bones and flesh of my flesh.""*

So Eve was an afterthought on Jehovah's part, subsequent to the beasts of the field and birds of the air. As for the "miracle" of her formation, some of you may remember Dolly, a domestic sheep born in 1996. She was the first known mammal to be cloned from an adult somatic cell, that is, a cell that had differentiated into a body part or organ rather than being a germ cell. Dolly was cloned from a mammary gland cell, which proved that a single cell taken from a specific body part could recreate a whole individual. Dolly lived for six and a half years before dying of a lung disease. Life expectancy for this breed of sheep is between twelve and fifteen years. The donor of the mammary cell was a six-year-old sheep, so Dolly's organs and body parts were six years old at her birth; therefore her death was not premature. Neither was the lung disease unusual. It is common among that breed of sheep.

> <u>Genesis 3:9</u>
> *"And Jehovah God kept calling to the man and saying to him: 'Where are you?'"*

This demonstrates that Jehovah was/is not omniscient or all knowing.

> <u>Genesis 3:21</u>
> *"And Jehovah God proceeded to make long garments of skin for Adam and for his wife and to clothe them."*

This demonstrates how actively and hands-on Jehovah was involved with Adam and Eve, much like a caregiver.

> <u>Genesis 3:22</u>
> *"And Jehovah God went on to say: 'Here the man has become like one of us in knowing good and evil.'"*

The comment "one of us" demonstrates that there were others like Jehovah. He was not a singular entity. God is singular.

> <u>Genesis 4:1</u>
> *"Now Adam had intercourse with Eve his wife and she became pregnant. In time she gave birth to Cain and said 'I have acquired a man with the aid of Jehovah.'"*

The same verse from the KJV reads,

> "And Adam knew Eve his wife; and she conceived, and bare Cain, and said, 'I have gotten a man from the Lord.'"

These comments had earlier eluded my attention until I noticed a pattern of dependency upon Jehovah for conception among the wives of the major patriarchs of Adam's descendants. Here is Eve saying the same thing: she had gotten sons with the help of Jehovah.

Moving down the line, Abraham's half-sister, Sarah, became his wife and was barren until when into her nineties, she conceived and bore their son, Isaac, according to Jehovah's prediction. Isaac married his cousin Rebekah who was barren until Jehovah opened her womb, and she gave birth to twins. One of the twins, Jacob, married his mother's kinsman, Rachel, who was barren until Jehovah opened her womb twice, and she bore two sons, Joseph and Benjamin.

Jacob, whose name was changed to Israel by Jehovah, took the Israelites into Egypt. His son, Joseph, whose brothers sold him to a passing caravan of traders, went from slave to overlord in Egypt and saved Egypt from starvation.

Going forward in time to the New Testament era, Elizabeth, the mother of John the Baptist, was barren and old when she gave birth as Jehovah had said that she would. And of course Mary was a virgin when she conceived and gave birth to Jesus. These facts clearly indicate that Jehovah was involved in genetic manipulation and gynecological practices. Jehovah was building a bloodline that would lead to the birth of a Jewish king who would rule the world.

> Genesis 5:23-24
>
> "So, all the days of Enoch amounted to three hundred and sixty-five years. And Enoch kept walking with the [true] God. Then he was no more, for God took him." — NWT
>
> "And all the days of Enoch were three hundred sixty and five years: And Enoch walked with God: and he was not; for God took him." — KJV

The patriarchs listed before Enoch and those listed after him all died. Enoch was taken. This declaration opens the door for interpretation. I have previously stated my own. Enoch was a prophet. See *Jude* verse 14. As a prophet, he apparently received preferential treatment.

The following speaks for itself:

> Genesis 6:4, KJV
> *"There were giants in the earth in those days; and also after that, when the sons of God came in unto the daughters of men, and they bare children to them, the same became mighty men which were of old, men of renown."*

Clearly, two different life forms have combined to produce a hybrid race, the Nephilim (see NWT).

> Numbers 13:33
> *"And there we saw the Nephilim, the sons of Anak, who are from the Nephilim; so that we became in our own eyes like grasshoppers, and the same way we became in their eyes."*

> Deuteronomy 1:28
> *". . . and also the sons of the Anakim we saw there."*

These populations of powerful giants were among the inhabitants of the lands of Canaan that Joshua and the Israelites had to deal with, to conquer and destroy on their way to the Promised Land. This passage clearly states that the sons of God had sexual intercourse with the daughters of men, which resulted in offspring. Sons of God? Were they angels? It is generally accepted that angels are sexless, therefore we are not talking about angels here. And the children of these unions were not angels; they were *"mighty men … men of renown."*

> Genesis 6:6-7
>
> *"And Jehovah felt regrets that he had made men in the earth, and he felt hurt at his heart. So Jehovah said: 'I am going to wipe men whom I have created off the surface of the ground, from man to domestic animal, to moving animal and to flying creature of the heavens, because I do regret that I have made them.'"*

To feel regret is a human emotion. To willfully destroy life is less than human. Could either of these qualities be assigned to God, the giver of life?

In the first place, I do believe in miracles. I have experienced miracles in my life. I bring up the following verses merely to reinforce the claim that not all events in the Bible that are considered miracles were miracles; rather, most were the result of natural phenomenon. Jehovah had just promised Moses that he would never again cause a flood to destroy the earth.

> *"My rainbow I do give in the cloud, and it must serve as a sign of the covenant between me and the earth. And it shall occur that when I bring a cloud over the earth, then the rainbow will certainly appear in the cloud."* Genesis 9:13-14

The church treats the appearance of the rainbow as a miracle or at least an astonishing feat on the part of Jehovah. But understanding a rainbow is just middle-school science. A specifically shaped crystal-like object called a prism when held a certain way will show us that light actually is made up of seven basic colors that the unaided eye does not perceive. We don't see the colors until the ray of light is bent or refracted, spreading the colors apart. When rays of light strike drops of moisture, the moisture acts as the prism, and a rainbow effect is produced. Jehovah was not performing a miracle; he was simply pointing out a natural occurrence that would serve as a reminder to man that the earth would never be destroyed by water again. The church finds great relief in this pronouncement, but instead lives in fear of the final form of total annihilation—fire.

(*Genesis* 11:1-9) This is the very interesting story of the *Tower of Babel*. Following the flood, Noah's three sons began to produce large families so that the descendants of Adam (they had not yet been given the name Israelites) were becoming very numerous and widespread. Remember these people began in Eden from which their forefather, Adam, had been cast out. They had no fixed location to call a homeland. Also, after the flood, they had to start the bloodline over again. These were Jehovah's chosen people.

Noah became a farmer, but as his sons began to multiply, they also began to spread out and adopt a nomadic lifestyle. They began to desire to put down roots, to settle down in one place. This is when Jehovah became alarmed. His subjects were becoming less and less dependent on him. So he caused them to begin speaking various languages, which forced them to scatter and to move off into smaller groups and go back to a nomadic existence. This put an end to their efforts to establish a homeland for themselves.

> Verse 1:
> *"Now all the earth continued to be of one language and of one set of words."*
>
> Verse 4:
> *"They now said: 'Come on! Let us build ourselves a city and also a tower with its top in the heavens, and let us make a celebrated name for ourselves, for fear we may be scattered over all the surface of the earth.'"*
>
> Verse 6:
> *"After that Jehovah said: 'Look! They are one people and there is one language for them all, and this is what they start to do. Why, now there is nothing that they may not have in mind to do that will be unattainable for them.*

Verse 7:

"Come now! Let us go down and there confuse their language that they may not listen to one another's language.'

Verse 9:

"That is why its name was called Babel, because there Jehovah had confused the language of all the earth, and Jehovah had scattered them from there over all the surface of the earth."

There's that phrase again, "all the earth." We know that by this time, mankind was scattered all over the earth, literally, so there were many languages being spoken at this period of time. Just as with the account of the flood, the phrase "all the earth" was referring to a relatively small geographical area.

I can postulate how the separation into various languages could have been achieved. Mass hypnotism or mind control is a very powerful tool and it is very real. Our governments know all about mind control-hypnotism, brainwashing, etc. Based on various books and documentaries I have seen regarding various government projects and programs, mind control is in wide use today and could easily have been utilized in biblical times by someone knowledgeable enough to use it.

(*Ezekiel*, Chapter 1) One of the most often-told biblical accounts used for suggesting alien presence is *Ezekiel's wheel* or chariot. It is also one of the most frequent targets of debunkers. Ezekiel was an Old Testament prophet. He was in close contact with Jehovah. Through Ezekiel, Jehovah sent many warnings and dire prophecies to his wayward subjects, the Israelites. The trick to making any sense of Ezekiel's sightings is to determine which aspects are visions and which are visuals. It must be obvious that much of what he "sees" is the product of an altered state of mind or a vision. Among the plethora of interpretations, there are those who envision luminous ethereal beings, and there are those who see symbolism: man, lion, oxen, and eagle are seen symbolically. But there are certain aspects of Ezekiel's description of what he saw that, in my mind, cannot be misunderstood and must be seriously considered for they definitely describe a material object and mechanical processes that are commonly described today by observers of unexplainable sightings.

From the *New King James Version*, Ezekiel 1: 4:
"Then I looked, and behold, a whirlwind was coming out of the north, a great cloud with raging fire engulfing itself; and brightness was all around it and radiating out of its midst like the color of amber."

Verse 7:
"Their legs were straight, and the soles of their feet were like the soles of calves' feet."

Verse 13:
"As for the likeness of the living creatures, their appearance was like burning coals of fire, like the appearance of torches going back and forth. The fire was bright, and out of the fire went lightning."

Verses 15-16:
"Now as I looked at the living creatures, behold, a wheel was on the earth beside each … as it were, a wheel in the middle of a wheel."

Verse 17:
"When they moved they went toward any one of four directions; they did not turn aside when they went."

Verse 18:
"As for their rims … their rims were full of eyes, all around…"

Verses 19-20:
"When the living creatures went, the wheels went beside them; and when the living creatures were lifted up from the earth, the wheels were lifted up … for the spirit of the living creatures was in the wheel."

Verse 24:
"When they went, I heard the noise of their wings, like the noise of many waters …"

I had planned to comment on each of the above verses but have decided that it is not necessary. I will, however, comment on the wheel within a wheel because "the spirit of the living creatures was in the wheel." In other words, the object was under the control of the wheels within the wheels.

When I was a child, I had a wheel within a wheel. It was called a gyroscope. Some of you will remember these spinning, top-like objects. It seems obvious to me that Ezekiel's wheels within wheels were the mechanisms by which the object changed speed and direction of movement. It could move from a stationary position in any direction and even up and down without turning or banking. A great cloud, straight legs with hoof-like feet, torches going back and forth, rims with eyes, fire and lightning, wind and noise—what does it take to convince one that Ezekiel was witnessing a flying craft of some kind, an airborne craft? An airborne craft during biblical times: What's the explanation? I think that it has been sufficiently demonstrated that the Bible does indeed contain suggestions, actually, clues that with regard to Jehovah, we are looking at alien intervention.

Whether Jehovah was/is a fallen angel or an alien being, he is certainly not the God who created man, the earth, and all upon the face of the earth. How long must God wait for mankind to recognize and embrace Him as He actually is? How many lifetimes does man need in order to emulate the very one who gave him being? God wants nothing more or less than to have mankind live together and love each other unconditionally even as He loves the whole of mankind unconditionally. How long must He wait?

GOD, PART THREE

God is not a mystery.
He does not hide his countenance from man.

When I was young, my family attended Bible study lessons every Sunday morning and again the same night. These lessons were not organized by the layman doing the teaching or by the church to which we belonged but by the governing body of all Baptist churches in the South. We actually had textbooks that we studied before classes. Rather than starting at the beginning and working our way through the Bible, we were given a broad overview of the key events and characters that the governing board deemed important.

The gory details of the Old Testament were circumvented for the most part, and the New Testament teachings were centered about Jesus and the gospels and tended to exclude the letters and admonitions of Paul and the lesser disciples. We were made keenly aware of the two possibilities for Christians—accept Jesus (as God) and go to Heaven or deny Jesus and go to Hell. The requirement was to accept what we were being told without question because there was only one way to obtain eternal life, and the church was telling us the way. There was no other.

But inevitably, questions did arise such as, "Did God really make the world in just seven days?" Answer: "God's time is not the same as man's time." That sounded reasonable to me. Another question was, "Who did Adam and Eve's sons marry?" Answer: "They married their sisters." Again, though distasteful, the explanation was reasonable.

But then there came the really tough questions: Since God is all loving and all forgiving,

"Why did God cast Adam and Eve out of the Garden of Eden?"

"Why did God destroy the whole world and all of mankind with the flood?"

"Why did God command Abraham to sacrifice his son?"

"Why did God harden the heart of the Egyptian pharaoh and cause so much unnecessary pain, suffering, and death prior to the exodus?"

"Why did God make the Israelites wander in the desert for forty years before entering the Promised Land?"

"Why did God sanction the slaughter of the inhabitants, even the animals of the city of Jericho in order to give their land to the Israelites?"

"Why did God not let Moses enter the Promised Land and, in fact, cause Moses to die before his natural time to die had come?"

You might think that there were no reasonable answers to these questions but there was one. The answer: "God is a mystery, and we are not meant to know his ways." When I was young, I thought that was a copout. Now, sixty years later, I know that it was a copout.

When I was young, I could not understand why God—the God I loved and who loved me and forgave all sins—could be so cruel. Now, as an adult I understand. I understand that God cannot be so cruel. God is incapable of cruelty. So, it is apparent that that was not God at work.

My understanding today is that God does not test, tempt, or punish man. When bad things happen, it is not God behind it. Nor does He just sit back and allow bad things to happen as so many dedicated Christians believe but through faith humbly accept. It is not God behind negative events in our lives. It is the laws of nature at work often coupled with man's interference and poor judgment. God, for the most part, is not engaged in our lives in a manipulative way.

What about positive intervention? Does God intervene in positive ways? I believe he does. It sounds like a contradiction on my part. It is a contradiction on my part and one that I cannot explain. For some reason, I cannot blame God for negatives in life, but I can and do thank Him for the positives, even sometimes "miracles."

We cannot know the mind of God, but He does make Himself known to us by surrounding us with his spirit. It can be seen, heard, and sensed in numerous ways simply by looking around and by contemplating life in the simplest of terms. God is not a mystery. He is in every breath we take, the beating of our hearts, the functioning of our minds and of our imaginations. His spirit resides in our souls.

The truth that all mankind should be able to accept is that God does exist and that God is the purest and only example of perfection. Consider the following:

What God Is

God has always been and will always be.

God is the source of the whole of existence.

The essence that is God is omnipotent or all-powerful, omniscient or all-knowing and omnipresent or everywhere.

In God, the capacity for error does not exist.

God is supremely natural, and in no way is God supernatural.

God is a continuous and continuing revelation, not a mystery.

God is life, and in God, there is no such condition as death.

God is light, and in God, there is no darkness.

God is love, understanding, and forgiveness in the most complete and perfect sense.

What God Is Not:

God is not a tempter. He does not test human frailties.

God does not withhold favors from some while granting favors to others.

God has not chosen one man over another or one race over another.

All are equal in the mind of God.

God does not experience regret or remorse for He has made no mistakes.

God does not require the sacrifice of flesh or the letting of blood.

God does not require the sacrifice of material things.

God does not punish or inflict hardship, illness, injury, or pain.

God does not kill. He does not destroy that which He has made.

GOD PART FOUR

The Many Faces of God

Before going any farther, I need to apologize to all of the religions of the world that I have no knowledge of and therefore cannot reference in this writing. I can address only those religions that have touched my life personally. In addition to Protestant Christianity, I know of, but very little technically, Catholicism, Mormonism, Judaism, and Islam. I was born into and raised in a Protestant Christian church, so the reader must remember that I am writing from that perspective, from the things I was taught as a child and either continue to adhere to or, sadly, have put aside.

One of the most dedicated activities of the Christian church is missionary work. Many Christians, both Protestant and Catholic, have dedicated their lives to mission activity and many of these to the point of martyrdom. As a youth, I thought that mission work was important because, according to what I was being taught, anyone who had not accepted Jesus Christ as their savior would not be granted eternal life, even those who had had no opportunity to learn of him. That really upset me!

I thought of all the people living in really remote areas such as the deepest, darkest regions of the African and South American jungles, high inaccessible mountainous areas, etc. Many of these people have no knowledge of anything that exists outside their own small world. Do my Christian brethren actually believe that God will ignore, literally disown these innocent people? Apparently, yes thus the need for missionaries to save the lost by introducing them to God and specifically to Jesus Christ. Missionaries are generally loving, empathetic individuals who are willing to give up their own comforts and safe environments in order to "save the lost." Protestant and Catholic missionaries carry the message that there is one God and no other. Beyond all doubt, this is true. But which of the gods is the real God? Now there's the rub. How are we to know?

If I believe that there is just one God, then why do I speak of gods? Well, it seems that every religious sect has its own version of God. I have discovered that several religious sects not only share the same God, inadvertently, but share the same prophets and other main figures, yet are very divergent in their practices and beliefs. For example, Judaism, Christianity, and Islam all share many of the same players. I will briefly summarize the basics of these three very different but seemingly parallel religions. And please keep in mind that I am not an authority, not a scholar with regard to religious history, philosophy or theology. I have just a basic knowledge and understanding in that regard. But I do know that, speaking logically, two of these three must be thinking erroneously or possibly all three are. Somewhere along the line, truth has been perverted. When I say truth, I mean reality. Reality has become lost in these religions to mystery, myth, and fear.

Judaism

I have wondered if the Christian *Pentateuch* (the first five books of the Old Testament) and its counterpart in the Hebrew version, the *Chumash,* relate the same record. I have not read the Jewish scriptures or even a translation of them, but according to what I have been able to find from reliable sources on the Internet, they do. There are certainly differences in the use of words and the spelling of words, but they do tell the same story.

I have been curious to know just when Judaism began and what it teaches about the origin of man. The only thing I have been able to find out (from the Internet) is the claim is that Judaism began with the man Abraham who, with his contemporaries, was the first to become known as "the people of one god." Yet the first mention of Abraham's forebears tells, in the book of *Genesis,* of the formation of the first of their race over nineteen hundred years earlier. That person was the man Adam who was formed from the "dust of the ground."

I assume that Judaism, like Christianity, embraces the myth that Adam was the first man. At least that is what I was allowed to believe as a child. This brings us to the inevitable question that all of us have queried: Who did Adam's sons marry? There seem to be variations within Judaism and Christianity, but the general belief is that his sons married their sisters. Today, that is known as incest, which often produces mental and physical defects in the resulting offspring. It is not an acceptable practice today.

For my part, I believe that the man Adam was an actual historical figure and the father of the race of people who were to become known as Israelites who have become known as Jews. So he was the first *of his kind*. In my research, I discovered that the written accounts of Adam and his descendants, as recorded in the books of *Genesis* and *Exodus*, are precise with regard to data. The accounting of the early history, as it is written and without alteration or supposition, ties into recorded world history in the year 586 BCE when King Nebuchadnezzar of Babylon destroyed the temple in Jerusalem and captured the last Israelite king, Zedekiah. This is both biblical and historical fact.

For comparison, when we discuss Islam and Christianity, I have listed the main and most critical characters in Judaism in ascending order as recorded in *Genesis* and *Exodus:*

Adam: The first member of the race that became known as Israelites. Was Adam the first man or the first of his race?

Enoch: The seventh from Adam, the first prophet and the first to "walk with god" who did not die but was "taken" by Jehovah.

Noah: The ninth from Adam who, with his sons, saved the race by surviving the flood and propagating the race.

Abraham: The nineteenth from Adam who represents the beginning of monotheism and of whom Jehovah promised to make a great nation and to give the "Promised Land" for a home.

Jacob: The twenty-first from Adam twenty-one hundred years later whose name was changed to Israel and who, with his twelve sons, greatly enlarged their numbers and became the slave force in Egypt.

Moses: Who rescued the Israelites from Egypt and to whom Jehovah gave the Hebrew law and the Ten Commandments.

Jesus: The Jewish prophet and teacher born circa 4BCE-4CE whom Judaism rejects as the Messiah and whose teachings became the basis for Christianity. (See *Matthew* 2:14-15 re Jesus' birth. The date of Herod's death is argued. Best source is 1 B.C.)

This brings us to the most important figure in the early history of the Israelites—Jehovah. When Moses asked god to identify himself by name, the reply, according to *the New World Translation of the Holy Scriptures*, was Jehovah. The term Jehovah is a relatively recent form that seems to have been transcribed from the base form YHWH. The *King James Version* of the *Holy Bible* uses the term Jehovah only seven times, using instead the terms Lord or Lord God. Ancient Hebrew had no vowels and there is no J in the Hebrew language, so you can easily see that the term is the invention of later scribes. The word "hovah" in Hebrew means "ruin" or "disaster," so it would seem that the term or name Jehovah would not be a desirable one to have or be given.

As it stands, the Hebrew language has many names for God such as Yah, Yahu, Yeho, Adonai, Eloah, Elohim, and others. One of the most readily recognized is Yahweh. Even though it was the use of the term Jehovah that alerted me to the fact that Jehovah is not God the Creator, it is not the name I am concerned with. It is the character of the entity that was/is Jehovah. The word "hovah" (ruin and disaster) does indeed seem appropriate for him. As has been previously stated, Jehovah simply does not meet the requirements of moral character, of mercy and goodness, of infallibility that define God the Creator. Maybe the ancient scribes were correct in their choice of the root word "hovah." By his own words, Jehovah is a *"manly god, a god of war,"* not a god of infinite love and mercy and forgiveness as is God the Creator.

It is the firm belief of Judaism that Israel (Hebrews, Semites, Jews) is the favored, the chosen race of their god, entitled to rule the world. I believe that this is partly true. Israel is the chosen race of Jehovah; by some means, they were created by Jehovah, but they are not entitled to rule the world. The world belongs to God the Creator. The world was created for all of mankind, not for a single race.

As an ideology and in consideration of my limited knowledge of the religion, I personally find no critical fault in Judaism other than they believe that Jews are the only humans that God loves so are destined to rule the world. What nonsense! Then of course there is the other thing—they worship a false god, Yahweh, Jehovah.

Islam

I have just recently begun looking into the religion of Islam, and the most critical thing I learned is that, for every question raised, inevitably there are divergent opinions and diametrically opposed explanations. Of course this is also true of Judaism and Christianity. It is the nature of the beast, the beast being the attempt to interpret or explain anything of antiquity for which there is no undeniably authentic record. Individual and thereby opposing views are a given. For example consider the following opposing statements: Muhammad wrote the Qur'an vs. Muhammad was illiterate and could not have written the Qur'an. But it seems that both of these statements are probably true.

From what I have been able to discover, I think that the story is: Seeking answers to life, Muhammad went into isolation to meditate and had a vision of God and Jesus standing side by side. On subsequent periods of meditation, an angel (Gabriel it is said) appeared to Muhammad and began revealing truths to him. Muhammad eventually disclosed the details of these visitations to his wife, Knadija, who, with the help of a male relative, began to write everything down. Additionally, Muhammad had followers who listened to his stories and recorded his accounts of his visions. Thus, the Qur'an came into being. Referring back to the above-mentioned opposing statements, if you change the word "wrote" in the first to "authored," the matter is resolved.

Islam as a sect is a newcomer having taken root in the sixth century CE. Amazingly, it closely parallels its forebears, Judaism and Christianity. In fact, whereas Christianity has stolen it "roots" from Judaism, it appears that Islam has basically stolen from both Judaism and Christianity, having added the twist of a new prophet, Muhammad.

Despite teaching that there have been thousands of prophets, Islam gives recognition to just twenty-five, with the first being Adam and the last

Muhammad. The most astonishing thing I discovered about Islam was that Islam has a Prophet Adam, the Adam of the *Genesis* account. However, I was also astonished and very happy to learn that Islam recognizes that there were men on Earth before the creation of Adam. Islam believes that Adam was the first of the population of Arabic nations. As in Judaism, Adam was formed by Allah (Hebrew, Yahweh) from the dust of the ground, from clay.

Before continuing, let me point out that in reading about Islam (as well as Judaism), names will often be spelled differently not only from between the languages but from one account to another within a language although they obviously refer to the same individuals. This being said, let me continue.

There are more than fifty characters mentioned in both the Torah, which is the Hebrew record, and the Qur'an, and at least four from both the New Testament of the Christian Bible and the Qur'an. Both Judaism and Christianity came before Islam, so what conclusion can we draw? Either Islam is a copycat version or the three religions are undeniably intertwined. The most notable shared figures are Adam, Idris (Enoch), Nuh or Nooh (Noah), Ibrahim (Abraham), Yaqub (Jacob), Musa (Moses), and Isa (Jesus). That Islam even recognizes Jesus as a prophet is a shock to me. And then we have Muhammad.

It appears that Muhammad is the most maligned figure among the supposed prophets. It has been said that he was a war monger, a murderer, a rapist, a pervert, a pedophile. Goodness me! How can so many millions of people find anything to admire about this person? He is scorned by many Christians for having taken a child bride, for being a pedophile. The child, Aisha, was around the age of nine when they married, though that figure has been disputed and has gone as high as fifteen. There is no proof whatsoever of her age. Muhammad was around the age of fifty. From historical accounts, Aisha was a very precocious young woman, very intelligent—and what we today would refer to as a type-A personality. It seems as though Aisha and Mohammad proved to be highly compatible both mentally and emotionally and were very happy together until he died. Muhammad advised his followers that after his death, they were to turn to Aisha for wisdom and guidance with regard to religious and other issues. She was largely responsible for the successful continuation of Islam.

I think it would be prudent if we enlighten ourselves as to the cultural norms for that day and time, which continue to this day in some countries. Taking children or very young women as brides was customary. Young children were betrothed at an early age. It was often years between the betrothal and the marriage. Then, too, a female child was considered a woman upon reaching puberty or attaining reproductive capability. It is not unheard of for girls of nine or ten to reach this stage of their development. A few have even given birth at this age.

Another issue that Christians like to use in criminalizing Muhammad is the claim that he was a war monger. In response to this, we are compelled to mention the battle for Jericho between the Israelites and the Canaanites, which was closely orchestrated by Jehovah. Upon gaining entry into the city, the Israelites murdered every man, woman, child, and beast they found there then burned the city to the ground. This was done so that they could occupy the land themselves. The destruction of Jericho was just the beginning of the Israelites' aggression toward other nations in their quest for land that they could call a homeland. Indeed, the Israelites were feared by all they came into contact with. Jehovah saw to that.

There is also the charge by many Christians that the only way Muhammad gained followers was by force. Those he conquered in battle were given the choice: convert to Islam or die. I would like to recall three instances recorded in the KJV of the Bible in the book of *Numbers*, Chapter 16. Remember there were approximately two million Israelites living in the desert after escaping from Egypt. Jehovah had begun presenting to them, through Moses, the laws and rules they were to live by. When they grew tired of their nomadic existence and of the burden of Jehovah's many demands, an assembly of two hundred and fifty princes of the house of Levi—one of the sons of Jacob—rose up against this treatment and against Moses by refusing to sacrifice to Jehovah. They were warned that disobedience would be punished. All who continued to side with the protestors were buried alive. The earth opened up and swallowed all of them along with their families and possessions. No visible trace of them remained. Then Jehovah went on to burn the two hundred and fifty princes alive.

Subsequently, when remaining Israelites spoke up against the atrocities that had taken place, Jehovah brought a plague upon them. Fourteen thousand and seven hundred people died. Could these actions be the actions of an all-forgiving God of love? No! These were the actions of an evil being. Have the outspoken Christians who make harsh charges against Muhammad even read their own holy book, the Bible? What is that verse we all like to recall on occasion? It goes something like "first remove the speck from your own eye."

It's like I said earlier, the events and players recorded in all three of the writings—the Torah, the Bible, and the Qur'an—are equally subject to discussion and debate. There is no hard-core proof that any of their theologies provide the definitive answer to the matters of God, man, and soul. One is forced to pick and choose which events, even which ideology is correct. In fact, they could all be incorrect. A person must follow his heart or, as I say, listen to his or her own soul. God will not judge one for staying true to the murmurings of his or her soul. It is the soul within us that harbors spiritual knowledge and is our true link to God.

I recently received an article that contained a letter by one hundred and twenty-six of the world's leading Islamic scholars that was sent to Abu Bakr al-Baghdadi, current head of the so-called Islamic States of Iraq and Syria (and of Isis), denouncing his claim to be a representative of Islam. The letter was quite long but was well worth reading. After reading it, I experienced a certain degree of relief regarding my fears about Islam based on the current happenings in the Middle East.

I can see that in its purest form, Islam is a religion of peace. According to these scholars and according to the correct interpretation of the Qur'an, Allah is not only merciful but is the infinite example of love, mercy, and forgiveness. Although warring is sometime necessary for self-preservation, murder is forbidden by Allah in any form for any reason. Also, if I have read correctly, it is against Islamic law to declare anyone to be a non-Muslim or to even inquire if he or she is Muslim or not.

Another surprising revelation was to learn that Allah does not smile upon martyrdom but looks upon it as an act of pride, of self-aggrandizement. It is an act that will not be rewarded. Also, women are not to be thought of as second class but are to be respected. This is quite a different picture from the one that we are being shown by the media and other religious groups. Who do we believe?

It became clear to me that radical, militant jihadists do not represent Islam. They don't know or understand the religion they claim to fight in the name of. They have perverted, actually bastardized the religion that they claim to represent. The really frightening thing is that these dark forces within Islam are recruiting young and vulnerable souls to their decadent way of thinking at an alarming rate. We all need to pray that God or Allah will intervene quickly to dispel the horror that is currently taking place in the Middle East and threatens the entire world.

I do hope the rest of the world can come to understand that law-abiding Muslims deserve our respect and concern. Sadly, it may be that Muslims also believe that they are the "chosen ones." I believe that the Muslim god, Allah, as presented in the true meaning of Islam is the same though misinterpreted God revered by Christianity and by most of the religions of the world and is, in fact, the God of us all. There really does need to be an awakening. Through constant dissention, man is threatening the spirituality of mankind.

Christianity

As I mentioned earlier, I was raised a Christian. I am a Christian. And for the record, I want to state that I do believe that Jesus lived and made it his mission to enlighten man as to the existence and true nature of God and man. And further, that he was murdered by his own race for his efforts, dying for the ideology that Christianity is based on—that there is one God who created all and who has ordained the possibility of everlasting life for the whole of mankind. I believe that the only way we will not experience everlasting life is by choice, by the willful drawing away from the essence that is God that resides in us all. I believe in miracles, and I believe in angels. I also believe in the laws of nature that God has put into place.

I mentioned that as an established religion Islam is relatively young. It is the same with Christianity, which is just a few hundred years older than

Islam. On the other hand, Judaism, or the basis of Judaism and its history, goes back more than six thousand years. From what I can see, both Islam and Christianity depend wholly upon the history of the Israelites, beginning with the creation of Adam as the foundation for their beliefs with each having added their own avatars, prophets, saints, events, and laws.

The history of Christianity begins with the birth of its avatar, the man Jesus. Christianity believes that Jesus was/is the Messiah that was prophesied in the Hebrew scriptures of Judaism. In fact, Jesus's birth, life, and death fulfilled hundreds of Hebrew prophesies of a coming Messiah. Yet Judaism rejects Jesus as the Messiah. Why? The Jews were expecting a king, one who would rule the earthly world and establish Judaism worldwide. Jesus was anything but a king, and he blatantly disregarded Jewish law.

What is known about Jesus's life is scant and what is taught is largely speculation. In *Zealot* by Reza Aslan (it is well worth reading—a very good presentation of Jesus and his times), we are told that Jesus was illiterate. I personally do not agree with this. Had he not been able to read, he would not have been able to refer to parts of the Hebrew writings as he did. And I have read that during the "lost years" of his life, he actually traveled widely, studying various cultures and belief systems, and he studied with the Essenes, a Jewish sect of ascetics and mystics that existed from 200 BCE to 200 CE. Yet Jesus did not leave a single written word and did not attempt to establish a new religion. He was all about spreading the knowledge of the reality of God and man's relationship to God, and of the reality of eternal life. In this respect, Jesus was a savior and is a savior to this day. Many have turned to God due to the examples and teachings of Jesus.

And this brings me to the first parting of the way that I have with Christianity, which teaches that the only way to have eternal life is to accept the fact that Jesus's death made all our sins go away and secured for us everlasting life. The operative word or words here are: *the only way*. I have already expressed my non-acceptance of this belief. There are just too many of God's sons and daughters who will never hear of Jesus and others who simply cannot accept the Christian interpretation. There are many paths to God.

The second parting of the way is the fact that Christianity teaches that

Jesus is God himself, God come down to Earth. This is based on the doctrine of the Trinity, the three-in-one-god, God the Father, God the Son, and God the Holy Ghost. It has already been pointed out that this doctrine is straight out of ancient paganism. Time after time, Jesus stated that he was not God, his father. He often referred to himself as the son of God just as he often proclaimed himself to be the son of man. At any rate, he never once proclaimed to be God. I could offer verse after verse to illustrate that Jesus was man, not God, but you could counter with verse after verse that seems to say the opposite.

This is the nature of the New Testament of the Christian Bible that is the New Testament of the scriptures. There is so much contradictory information that it forces the reader to take sides. But I am going to quote several verses of scripture, which, to me, support with the utmost clarity who Jesus was, and then I will put the subject of the divinity of Jesus to rest. Unless noted otherwise, I am quoting from the King James Version because I believe that it is the most widely used of the various versions of the New Testament.

> Matthew 16:13-17
> *When Jesus ... asked his disciples saying, "Whom do men say that I the Son of man am?" And they said, "some say that thou art John the Baptist: some, Elias; and others, Jeremias, or one of the prophets." He saith unto them, "But whom say ye that I am?" And Simon Peter answered and said, "Thou art the Christ, the Son of the living God." And Jesus answered and said unto him, "Blessed art thou, Simon Bar-jo-na: for flesh and blood hath not revealed it unto thee, but my Father which is in heaven."*

<u>John</u> 14:8-12

Phillip saith unto him, "Lord shew us the Father, and it sufficeth us." Jesus saith unto him, "Have I been so long time with you, and yet hast thou not known me, Phillip? He that hath seen me hath seen the Father; and how sayest thou then, 'Shew us the father?' Believest thou not that I am in the Father, and the Father in me? The words that I speak unto you I speak not of myself: but the Father that dwelleth in me, he doeth the works. Believe me that I am in the Father, and the Father in me: or else believe me for the very works' sake. Verily, verily, I say unto you, He that believeth on me, the works that I do shall he do also; and greater works than these shall he do; because I go unto my Father."

<u>Mark</u> 16:19 NWT

So, then, the Lord Jesus, after having spoken to them, was taken up to heaven and sat down at the right hand of God.

<u>John</u> 5:30

"I can of mine own self do nothing: as I hear, I judge: and my judgment is just; because I seek not mine own will, but the will of the Father which hath sent me."

If these verses do not do it for you, do not enable you to separate Jesus from God, then try this little trick: The next time you hear or read anything about God, try substituting the word Jesus for the word God. I think then that the separateness will become clear for you.

Jesus's lineage is of utmost importance both to Christianity and to Judaism. It is essential to both religions that Jesus be of the House of David who was the second king to rule the Israelites. Two genealogies are given for Jesus in the New Testament. One is in *Matthew* 1:1-16 KJV and the other is in *Luke* 3:23-38 KJV. They do not agree, yet both are presented as terminating with Joseph, who, after all, was really not the father of Jesus. One is generated from David's son Solomon and the other from David's son Nathan, yet both follow the lineage from Judah, one of the twelve sons (and tribes) of Jacob (Israel). I have read that the genealogy given in *Luke* is Jesus's mother, Mary's genealogy although her name is not mentioned. This will have to be the case if we are to connect Jesus to the House of David; otherwise we are not given Jesus's lineage in the Bible.

Explanations for the virgin birth, for the claim that Jesus is God, that he is the messiah or is not the messiah are so numerous, variable, and convoluted that we will not pursue further these aspects of the man Jesus. I will however express my own simplified theory of who Jesus was. We have already mentioned that Jesus's birth fulfilled over one hundred Old Testament prophesies, yet Judaism does not accept him as the Messiah that was prophesied. They expected a king, but Jesus was anything but.

Jesus was to have been a perfect being, not born of woman but formed by God, as was Adam. Yet Jesus was born of woman. I suspect that the "immaculate conception" was planned and carried out by Jehovah, just as he had manipulated childbirth among Adam's descendants since the time of Eve. Jesus was to have been a king. But it was God who thwarted Jehovah's plan for Jesus when, upon his being born, the physical baby Jesus embraced and accepted God's offering, the enlightened soul of God's only begotten son. On more than one occasion, Jehovah attempted to draw Jesus back into his scheme, but Jesus was not swayed by Jehovah's tempting. Jesus recognized Jehovah for what he was: an evil entity and a corrupter of man.

I believe my explanation is a reasonable one. But it is also possible that God ordained the virgin birth and did so in a time and place so that Old Testament predictions would be fulfilled. But again, it is my own interpretation. To believe or not believe that biblical events actually happened is a matter of choice. There are no definitive answers, but we can believe that Jesus was a flesh and blood man, a historical figure.

I feel it is imperative to discuss the New Testament itself since it is the testimony of Christianity. A large part of the New Testament was penned by the convert Paul. A Jew by birth, Paul of Tarsus was a Roman by citizenry. He was greatly influenced by the Greek culture that was in vogue at the time, and he was a Christian because he was a follower of the teachings of Jesus and his early disciples. Paul was largely responsible for the success of the early Christian church. But since Jesus and his disciples left no Christian law, Paul looked largely to the laws of Judaism for his approach to life. And it was a very rigid approach with many do's and do not's. Christianity ignores most of his rules for living.

Although Christianity acknowledges the commandments that were given to Moses by Jehovah to be Christian "law," it blatantly disregards them. And as far as moral standards such as the overuse of alcohol and other destructive habit-forming substances, premarital and extramarital sex, divorce, unnatural couplings, unnecessary termination of in utero life, etc. go, Christians on the whole have become very complacent. Understandably, these are conditions of life brought on by individual upbringings and circumstances, but the point here is that these things are preached against yet participated in seemingly without breach of conscience. While not "sins," these are deterrents to soul growth.

Look at some of the religious practices of Christianity. We celebrate December 25 as the birth date of Jesus, yet we know that he was born in the springtime, not the month of December. In the spring when we celebrate Jesus's resurrection from death, we take our children from the church to the park to look for colorfully decorated eggs and pass out chocolate bunnies and sugar-coated chicks—all suggestive of fertility. Could anything be more pagan than this, more sacrilegious, more hypocritical?

I could go on and on but to what end? I know this for sure, that nothing you read or hear about religion and specifically the three religions discussed here is "written in stone." Those educated in these matters cannot agree on anything because for every opinion or "statement of fact," there is a contradictory opinion or supposition. The dozens of notes at the back of the aforementioned book, *Zealot*, are a testimony to this statement.

In the end, it is all a matter of individual interpretation. And also in the end, it just does not matter who, if anyone, is correct. The realities of our existence are constant and are in no way affected by the interpretations of man. Man's interpretations of what is real and what is not real do, however, affect not only his own but others' quality of life and soul condition. This is why we must be careful who we choose to follow. Follow your heart. Listen to your soul; it is the "voice" of God speaking to you.

No one knows positively who wrote each and every component of the Christian New Testament, or whether it is accurate or mere fiction or whether part truth and part fiction. A great many facts are known, but also, a great deal of supposition surrounds the history of the New Testament and of the personalities and events involved in its making. Various authors wrote from their own perspective based on facts they had been given or stories they had heard. We must remember this: history books are written around facts yet from the viewpoint of their writers or of the institution commissioning the writing.

Personally, I believe that Jesus was a man whose soul relinquished its divinity voluntarily in accordance with God's perfect plan and entered into the physical world for the purpose of pointing wayward souls (all of us) to God. Jesus himself became a less than perfect soul and as such was required to seek the state of perfection that is necessary for a soul to enter the divine realm where God abides. By his life and by his death—the ultimate sacrifice, because he submitted to the will of God—he was restored to his position at the right hand of God, the position he had occupied from the beginning and occupies today.

Talmud: "Who is wise? One who learns from <u>all</u>."

The Bible, KJV, <u>John</u> 3:17
"For God sent not his Son into the world to condemn the world; but that the world through him might be saved."

The *Qur'an* 5:48
"If God had so willed, he would have made all of you one community, but he has not done so, in order that he may test you according to what he has given you; so compete in goodness. To God shall you all return, and he will tell you the truth about what you have been disputing."

It seems to me that rather than being the means to salvation, religion has become the bane of the world.

Setting religion aside, who among us cannot relate to the following?

> Consider the day as it reveals the world,
> and the night that veils it in darkness.
> Consider the sky and its wonderful composition,
> the earth and its expanse.
> Consider the human self and He Who perfected it.
> And how He imbued it with awareness
> of what is right and wrong.
> The one who helps this self to grow in a clean way
> attains to happiness.
> The one who buries it in darkness is really lost.
> *Qur'an, The Sun*, 91: 1-10

GOD: PART FIVE

There is no God but God.

I recently read that there are only three explanations for life on Earth: Evolution, Aliens, God. The implication was that you must choose one of these three possibilities. I believe that all three explain life on Earth. But there is an order that must be accepted.

In the beginning, God first brought the earth, as well as the entire cosmos with its atmospheres and natural laws into being. God initiated the first spark of physical life on Earth. It may or may not have been a single, microscopic cell or organism. There could have been trillions of simple life forms and even some not so simple. We don't know. And we don't know exactly when, and we will never know how. The first chapter of *Genesis* in the Bible relates poetically the creative process in a natural order of appearance of the various physical bodies, elements, and life forms. The account is scientifically sound and utterly believable. Interpretation cannot change facts; nevertheless, yes, it is most definitely subject to interpretation.

Over eons of time, these life forms, eventually including man, began to change by way of adapting to the environment each existed in. This process is called evolution, a natural, scientific reality, not a mystical, fairy-tale-like process by which something is supernaturally changed. I believe, if we open our eyes, we can see evolution taking place in the here and now.

When I was in high school, of over one thousand students, there was a young man who towered over every other student. He was six foot four inches tall. Today, he would be of average height on any basketball team in the world. Not only are men getting taller but women are also increasing in stature. Six foot two or three and even taller is becoming commonplace among women athletes as well as non-athletes. Is this evolution at work? The third possibility—alien intervention—has already been discussed here. I firmly believe that alien beings found their way to Earth, observed our life forms, and saw that man was the dominant form. They proceeded to mingle their own DNA with that of man through the reproductive process resulting in the races of giants spoken of in the book of *Genesis*. They continued to experiment until they were able to artificially bring a man into being and then a woman. Initially, alien DNA allowed for very long life spans—longevity, necessary for intergalactic travel, was gradually out-bred once the aliens left Earth. They may return or may never return. Some believe that they are still among us.

In my mind, this is fact: Without God, life would not have begun, evolution would never have been set in motion, and visits from aliens would probably not have taken place, had they not first observed life on Earth.

If you choose to believe in God, the creative God, please choose not to pervert His character, those qualities that make Him God. Always keep in mind what God is and what God is not.

Once you can accept the fact that by His own design, the essence of God resides in you, you begin to be a better person. You just feel better about life, become more appreciative of the blessing that life is. Once you accept the fact that life on Earth, your individual life included, is moving according to God's perfect plan—and it is a perfect plan—you can relax and let God do the driving. Once you become able to say, "Not my will, God, but your will be done" and actually turn your life over to God, you will be amazed at how wonderful life can be. Don't expect perfection. That is not going to happen. But you can expect to experience a peace of mind that replaces the need or desire for understanding. You will begin to experience miracles in your life, literally. And most importantly, you will realize that physical death is not the end and that eternal life is the reality, for all.

There is no God but God

One God responsible for all things
One God for the entire family of mankind
One God who has ordained everlasting life for all who accept it
One God of perfect love
One God of infinite forgiveness
One God incapable of error
One God incapable of feeling remorse
One God incapable of desiring revenge
One God incapable of exacting hurt of any kind
One God possessing no ego
One God requiring no sacrifice
One God requiring no ritual praise
One God who loves us all
One God who waits for your soul

SOUL

Anima Immortalis

There is absolutely no scientific evidence supporting the existence of the human soul. Anything written about the soul has been gleaned from intuitive insights by way of meditation, prayer, epiphanies, mystical experiences, hypnosis, trances, near death experiences, etc. Any material of a factual nature written here has been borrowed from the interpretations of others who claim to be in the know. However, I have not written anything that I cannot agree on the possibility of. The only thing that I know for sure is that every human being has a soul. How do I know? My soul remembers. My soul remembers a time when it resided elsewhere and craves to return to that ethereal state of being one with the universe.

There are two forces at work in man: spirit and soul. They are not the same thing. Spirit is that essence of God that gives life to an otherwise lifeless body, the breath of life, so to speak. It is the animating force of all things physical. It is the sustainer of life. Man would like to and has tried to produce this force in his laboratories, but all he has been able to do is to harness and manipulate this force to some degree.

The other force within man is soul. I have likened the soul to the personality of God. The soul represents God's psyche. He has shared this facet of Himself with man in particular and with other organisms that are able to think and act independently as well. The soul represents the sum total of a person's individual characteristics, the person that he or she really is. The soul is not man's spirit but the spiritual aspect of man. It is the existence of the human soul, the spiritual nature of man that defines us and allows us to claim that we are made in the image of God.

Think of God as being a core of dynamic energy from which an infinite number of tiny sparks has burst outward—a starburst of energy. The mass of sparks forms a cohesive body, which, when taken as a whole, represents the Universal Soul. The Universal Soul is incorruptible and eternal. Every spark within the mass while it is not God is formed of the God essence, and each spark represents an individual soul. Each individual soul is given the capacity for individual thought as well as the freedom to think and act on its own. Those souls that wish to explore the physical universe must attach themselves to something physical in order to experience the physical world. The human body is the vehicle chosen by many souls.

The visible manifestation of the human soul is called the aura, a glow in the form of a halo that can be seen outlining the body. The aura is not visible to the "unseeing" eye. It is seen primarily by clairvoyants, psychics, and mystics. The glow takes on variable colors, which actually reveal the condition of the soul at any given time. God has given each soul complete freedom regarding the movements it makes and the paths it takes. With freedom comes choice, and with choice comes the possibility of error. As individual souls stray farther and farther from the universal gathering of souls, they begin to sense the separation and long to return. Each soul must find its own path back to its origin. This is the journey of the soul that every human must make—returning to the source from which it sprang. We all know that physical life is a temporary thing. But what lies beyond?

It is the soul within us that has retained the knowledge and the memories of our creation. It is the soul within us that prompts us to look within ourselves for answers to our existence. It is the soul that encourages us to seek answers, but ultimately, the goal of the soul is not merely to attain knowledge but to attain wisdom. As we gain knowledge through our memories and experiences, we must develop the wisdom to utilize that knowledge in the most appropriate way.

What is the best way to learn? We all know the proverbial answer to this question. The best way to learn is by experience. You may remember one of the laws of physics learned in school: For every action, there is an equal and opposite reaction. For every cause, there is an effect. Behind every effect lies a cause. These laws of nature apply to every aspect of our being. Think about this and you will realize just how important our day-to-day, moment-by-moment choices are. The choices we make determine the quality of our lives. When we make negative choices negative results follow. When we make positive choices, we enhance the quality of life. Yet even though we strive to make positive choices, negativity unfailingly creeps in. Why? It is due to the wisdom of the Universal Soul.

The Universal Soul does not create struggle and negativity in life, but it does understand the need for it and accepts it. The Universal Soul encourages each of us along paths that will encounter negativity or struggle because therein lies the potential for greater and more rapid soul growth. Struggle is not the punishment or testing of the soul. Struggle is meant to be the impetus that carries and keeps a soul moving along the right paths toward the perfection necessary for reunion with God. I think it is very important to stress that negatives in life are not God punishing or testing us. Negativity and positivity are simply the laws of nature at work, not God's interference.

In discussing the human soul, I want to state at the outset that what you read here is basically my own interpretation of this rather mystical aspect of man. I have read a fair amount of philosophical treatises concerning God, the human soul, and man's soul nature. Much of it has gone into my brain and out again, as the majority of it has been too convoluted and mystical for my western-influenced mentality.

What I would like to do is to paint a picture of the human soul as being a matter-of-fact reality as opposed to the soul being simply a philosophical enigma. The soul is not a temporary spirit form that resides somewhere inside us and hopefully goes to Heaven when our body dies. The soul is a spiritual entity with memory, intelligence, personality, feelings, and aspirations. The soul is the aspect of man that continues after physical death. Actually, it should be pointed out that there is no such thing as physical death, merely organic change from one form to another. But upon supposed physical death, the soul continues to exist. But where does it go?

We have said that souls originated when God cast His essence out into the universe, forming a mass of individual souls traveling together through space and time. Having been given the freedom to do so, many souls have strayed from confinement within the universal gathering. Many find their way to Earth. There are many physical life forms available to these spiritual entities for habitation. The most highly evolved and frequently sought after is man.

Let's stop thinking of the soul or souls as sparks but as actual spiritual entities, entities desiring "more." On earth, man is desperately imploring, "Who am I? Why am I here?" Men seeking spiritual answers, souls seeking physical experiences; *voila!* Yes, it sounds like something right out of *Grimm's*. But be charitable and suppose this scenario to be reasonable. Let's also be honest and admit that supposition is all that we have. Definitive answers to questions regarding the how, when, and why of mankind and of his soul will forever remain impenetrable by the human mind. Some may think they have the answers, but those who do are as fallible as you and I.

Now that we have the "mystery"—the unanswerable—out of the way, let's turn our attention to explanations that are both possible and reasonable regarding man and his soul. Science is now beginning to recognize that the soul probably does exist. Many reliable doctors have witnessed among their patients and even among themselves near-death experiences as well as medical phenomenon, "miraculous" healings, etc. But what we know or what we think we know about the human soul has been gleaned from revelations experienced by clairvoyants, those having keen insight, perception, or discernment. Actually, clairvoyance can be experienced by almost anyone and has in fact been experienced by many. Those who have experienced clairvoyance know that it is the real deal. Just ask them. They cannot be swayed from the belief that they have experienced true insight and been shown the rightful answers to great mysteries.

Clairvoyant studies tell us that there is a spiritual realm in which souls normally reside and await the opportunity to gain earthly experiences for the purpose of accelerating their return to the Godhead. This cannot be achieved in a single lifetime, so each soul experiences many lifetimes, in fact, as many as it takes to perfect itself. It experiences living in different genders, countries, races, religions, etc., for it is only by walking down many diverse paths that it can rise above the all too human characteristics of ignorance, prejudice, and hatred and move toward godliness.

A soul enters a body during or shortly before or after the physical birth of the body in which it chooses to reside. Yes, the soul makes the choice. Since it retains memories of past lives and accompanying shortfalls, the soul will choose the circumstances it is born into. It will choose those factors which will better help it attain spiritual growth. For example, if in its previous life, the soul railed against a certain race or religion, it will probably choose to come back as a participant in that particular race or religion. This way, it can experience firsthand the heartache of being the subject of bias or prejudice and hopefully overcome bias and prejudice in its own self. In a previous life, if a man has been a defiler of women, his soul may choose to come back into its present life as a woman who will be defiled. If in a previous life, a person has been a murderer, then his soul may choose to be murdered in its present life. Such choices are given to the soul to make. In making these choices however, the soul acts in harmony with the wisdom of the Universal Soul.

At this point, it should also be said that the soul determines its own exact time and manner of death. Don't confuse soul choice with mental willpower. Ultimately, willpower will relinquish its struggle against death. Soul choices supersede mental, physical choices. All choices, however, are subject to the overall blueprint of God's plan.

Individual souls function within groupings. Souls that were friends or relatives will move through multiple lifetimes as a unit but with varying relationships. And of course, there will be exceptions. This is one reason why we feel a deeper love for those who are close to us. With them, we have shared many lifetimes and are what is referred to as soul mates. As soul mates, we have a particular interest in the physical wellbeing and spiritual condition of those we love, and we will love more those with whom we have had previous relationships.

As far as individual souls go, clairvoyant studies tell us that there are six categories of souls: the physical, human, psychical, rational, illumined, and divine. The Greek word for soul is *psyche*. The Latin word for soul is *anima*.

The Physical Soul – *Anima bruta* - The Animal Soul

As has already been mentioned, souls desiring "more" have found their way to Earth and to humankind. At some point, a soul will become bored with the physical, material, limited way of earth life, will be reminded of the more desirable state from which it has emanated, and will begin to wish to return to that higher state. There are, however, souls for whom this desire is never ignited while here on Earth. There are souls that have separated from the spiritual nature of life and have begun to descend downward into the lower regions of physical or material existence. There are souls that are sinking downward into the base qualities of physical life, rather than moving upward toward the higher spiritual state. Such souls are unenlightened and full of psychic ill-health. At once, you may think of those imprisoned for their acts of murder, torture, robbery, etc. But all *anima bruta* are not found in prisons nor are all those found in prisons *anima bruta*.

Anima bruta or dark or descending souls are just as often found in human personalities that one would least suspect of harboring such an unenlightened soul. I personally believe that more than material goals such as wanting to be rich and famous, having the lust for power and control over others is the basest of desires and the ultimate example of spiritual descent. There are organized movements worldwide with goals to control the world. They plot disasters and events in order to eliminate certain groupings of people or to gain control over them. It is not just the self-proclaimed terrorist groups. Most crimes against mankind are carried out under the cloak of secrecy by those who are mistakenly trusted by the masses. Such organizations do exist and are not simply conspiracy theories as some would like to believe. Evil comes in varied forms and is always deceptive and self-serving—wolves in sheep's clothing.

The atrocities that some humans inflict upon others go beyond human understanding. Such souls have got to represent the bowel of humanity. Without doubt, these souls fall into the category of *anima bruta*. Their acts are often blamed on their upbringing or lack thereof. The defenses of early abuse, poverty, or discrimination in some form are often cited. These are not valid defenses as there are many who experience such negative forces yet transmute the negatives into positives, putting themselves well onto the upward path toward spiritual enlightenment.

Unenlightened *anima bruta* are spiraling downward into the depths of human existence. As I have previously stated, I have not attained the level of discernment necessary to know the possibilities or the outcome for such decadent souls. But I do believe, keeping with the understanding that God is all forgiving, that the courses of such souls can be changed in a heartbeat when and if the soul reaches out to its own spiritual nature and listens to and obeys its promptings.

Unfortunately, it seems that our world, the earth, has become saturated with souls of the *anima bruta* type. But the real heartache is how rapidly and thoroughly these souls are influencing younger, easily misled souls. And how is this being accomplished? Media and technology are making the assault on man's spiritual nature possible. But how do you stop "progress?" The decadent souls behind the corrupting of our youth and youthful souls are ensconced in their power to use and control. The way to stop these moguls, or mongrels, is to refuse their offerings. Only the youth themselves can do this. So let us all focus on and pray for an awakening among our youth.

The Human Soul – *Anima humana*

The humanizing of a soul occurs when it enters a newly born physical body. Under normal circumstances, that is, as long as there is no physical condition that prevents it, the soul is immediately bombarded by the reality of the five senses—sight, sound, smell, taste, and touch. Immediately, it is challenged by the urgency for the meeting of its various physical needs—warmth, nourishment, affection, comfort, protection, and thereby total dependency on others. It begins being influenced by the physical, material nature of the life it has chosen for itself.

At this early stage, the soul still clings to the memories of the experiences of past lives and of the elevated state from which it originated and from which it has just come. As Wordsworth phrased it, "Heaven lies about us in our infancy." But very quickly, the influence of worldly thought begins to fade these spiritual memories. As Wordsworth also observed, "Our birth is but a sleep and a forgetting." Also at this point, the pathway that will take it through its present earthly sojourn is activated. This path may or may not be the one to take it to its highest development while on Earth. Along this main path will be many smaller footpaths and detours and distractions and, yes, temptations. The soul will experience and must choose from a plethora of human influences that will either lift it toward spiritual realms or drag it earthward, depending on the choices that the soul makes.

Although it is primarily an individual's circumstances of birth and subsequent upbringing and environmental factors that affect a soul's passage through life, these things have no real power over the soul. It is the individual psyche that holds sway over a soul's choices. When the psyche leans toward excessive sensuality, materialistic goals, and worldly influences the soul becomes dull and darkened. On the other hand, the psyche can influence a soul to reach toward lofty pursuits and high ideals. These antithetical forces are constantly at odds within the psyche. But the psyche has another very important function. The psyche records and remembers past experiences both in the soul's current life and its former lives.

Deja vu—we have all experienced it—the feeling that we have been here before or done this before. Probably we have, and it is the psyche remembering it. A "brainstorm" that results in a positive outcome is probably the psyche at work. Innate talents in areas such as music, art, science, teaching, writing, and many others is the psyche remembering and drawing upon past skills developed in earlier lives and not forgotten. An unexplained liking for a person or place or an unexplained fear or disdain is the psyche remembering past relationships. Strong psychic and even physical bonds between two people are the result of psychic memory. The psyche of all men is rich with the memories of their past-life experiences.

The Rational Soul – *Anima ratione*

"The greatest honor God can bestow upon a soul is not to give to it great things, but to ask of it great things." —*St. Therese of Lisieux*

Conscience, ethics, character, morals, principles, beliefs, standards, convictions, faith, knowledge, wisdom—these are all components and concerns of the rational soul. And it is in these areas that so many souls begin to fade away or to stray.

The backbone of the rational soul is the conscience. Though there are undeniably some, very few humans lack a conscience. Those who lack a conscience are missing a crucial tool that is helpful, perhaps even necessary in steering the soul heavenward rather than earthward.

The conscience is man's authority to act, think, and believe as he so chooses. When man heeds and adheres to the urgings of his conscience, he need not depend on the opinions or advice of others. His conscience is the final test for all he thinks or does. If man listens to his conscience, he will not repeat mistakes made in previous existences.

The quality, which most outwardly reflects the condition of one's soul, is character. Character is a trait developed over many lifetimes and with vigorous effort. Character is an aspect of the soul that is easily sensed by others and is a trait that affords self-respect and faith in oneself.

The qualities mentioned above represent man's effort to reach out to the laws of the universe, to the godlike nature it innately possesses but that has become watered down in its desire for material experiences. This push toward godliness is born of an inner awakening of the soul and the knowledge that it has the task of qualifying itself for its return to God.

Sadly, this awakening in man to the existence of his higher self is usually slow in coming in any given lifetime. Man becomes so saturated in his material existence that matters of the soul are for the most part neglected. Eventually, when human testing becomes an unbearable burden, the soul arouses and reaches out to help and to be helped and a "rebirth" or an "illumination" does occur. Once the soul is recognized and allowed to exert itself in an individual's life, grand moments of insight and great strides toward spiritual understanding begin to happen.

Anima illuminati and *Anima divina* will not be discussed here. This author is not qualified to do so.

I do have one comment, however, in reference to the term *illuminati*. There is a world-wide gathering of worldly souls who apparently consider that they themselves have become illumined. You can be sure that it is not their soul condition that they are referencing. In fact, the soul condition of those member souls is severely in question, considering that their goal is world-wide domination—domination over the many by the few. It sounds a bit like some of the religions we have discussed. Members of certain of these organizations are among the most celebrated personalities. They appear to be great patriots of their individual countries and contributors to the wellbeing of society and seekers of world peace, but their goals are not peace and tranquility. They aspire to dominate and control the masses and that means every aspect of your life and the lives of your children and their children. Do not fall into their trap. Do not become their victims. Many, especially in the various fields of entertainment and journalism and literature, already have. Again, the youth can disrupt their plans by not partaking of their offerings.

REINCARNATION

Life after Life

With the gradual and inevitable ending of physical life, the soul begins to lose interest in earthly matters and physical attractions. As it is slowly released from this cycle of its being, and it prepares to abandon its physical form, the soul calls into mind all the events that have become the record of its present lifetime. Those persons who have had near-death experiences often report that their whole life flashed before their eyes. It is the sum of the present lifetime that the soul will take with it into the next life.

The next life: What is meant by the "next life"? For too many, there are only two possibilities after death—life in Heaven with God or life in Hell with Satan. If I believed this to be true, I would go out of my way to be a very, very, very good person. Of course there would have to be forgiveness for those not so good things I did before I was mature enough to judge between good and bad. And there would have to be forgiveness of the wrong things I have done since, not on purpose but due to weakness or to bad choices, or to unavoidable circumstances. And there will have to be forgiveness for the missteps I will make in the future. There will certainly be some.

I was baptized at the age of nine, and, from that point on, I have not worried about going to Hell. When I was young, it was because I had accepted the fact that Jesus had died for my sins and his blood has washed me clean; therefore, I would certainly go to Heaven. Now, in my old age, I still don't worry about going to Hell but for a different reason. I know that God has forgiven all of my sins but now I don't believe in Hell. I stopped believing in Hell years ago because I know that my God, due to His purity, has not ordained such an outcome for any soul, regardless of its condition. Hell is an invention of human minds. Although I have stopped believing in Hell, I most definitely believe in Heaven, though my expectations are not now what they were in my youth. Being in Heaven means simply being with God, and I have no idea what that is like except that it is a state of perfection, of complete happiness, a total release from worry and pain: utopia, paradise.

I used to hear the older adults talk about going to Heaven to its mansions and streets of gold, and, quite frankly, I was not impressed. I could think of nothing I would want less. Actually, I became concerned that I would be bored in Heaven. This was before the time when it became somewhat commonplace for people to talk about their near-death experiences and visits from deceased loved ones, a time when the idea of life after death was still a simple matter.

I was twenty-six, and it was weeks before the birth of my third child when a beloved aunt passed away in the prime of her life. During the memorial service for her, I became so profoundly affected by grief that I had to leave the service and go outside. It was a deeper grief than I had ever experienced. Also during the service, my godmother was called away. Her husband, my godfather who I was close to had had a heart attack at home. He did not survive the attack. Even though it was done out of concern for me, I have always bemoaned the fact that I was not told of his passing until after my child was born. I was not able to properly grieve for him. Weeks later after the birth of my child, I had an experience that I can define only as an epiphany.

On this particular night, I was unable to sleep. If I was kind, I would not say that it was due to my husband's snoring, but sometimes I am not kind. At any rate, I sought relief by going into our third bedroom, which we had furnished with twin beds for our boys, though they were still too young to sleep on beds without rails. The beds were parallel across from each other, one on the inside wall and the other on the outside wall of the room. I chose the one on the outside wall. There was a space between the curtain and the wall through which I could see the light from a lamppost up the street. As I gazed at the light, I became overcome with sorrow, thinking about my deceased aunt. I began to weep huge watery tears, which caused the light to intensify and pulsate.

The next thing that I was aware of was being in a bubble of some kind and the pressure within it was closing around me so tightly that I began to struggle to breathe. I thought I was dying. At the last possible moment, the bubble burst, the pressure was released and a message was given me. I did not hear a voice, rather the words were simply implanted in my mind. I was told that my aunt was my newborn's guardian angel. With that I opened my eyes and looked about the room. The bed I had originally been lying in was untouched, undisturbed, and I was now in the second bed. Apparently, I immediately had fallen asleep and did not stir further until morning. Even then, I did not think about the night before. You may not think that this was that earth-shaking an experience but for me, a science student, the unusual physical aspect had the effect of assuring me that I had had an unsolicited moment of spiritual insight. Shortly thereafter, I began my search into the subject of angels. This was the renewal of my search for truth, my spiritual journey.

Among Christians, the term and idea of guardian angels is easily accepted. We all know that we have guardian angels protecting us but these are filmy, illumined, winged beings who are lifelong residents of Heaven. They are not human personalities who have just recently made it there. So this is where my search began: the subject of guardian angels.

One of the first things that came to my attention was the idea of reincarnation. In that day in the environment in which I was raised, if that word had been mentioned, eyebrows would have raised and eyes rolled, mine included. No one wanted to believe that they would come back to life as a grasshopper or a worm or even something as beautiful as a bird or a flower. As I continued to delve into the subject, it did not take long before those fears were assuaged. Reincarnation, as it turns out, is a Godsend, a blessing.

As I continued to delve into matters of the soul and reincarnation, I began to see that my soul was much more than I had understood it to be. Not only did I really have a spiritual counterpart in having a soul, but I realized that my soul was the real me. I came to understand that my body was simply a vehicle housing my soul, enabling it to exist on the physical plane, and my mind was simply a tool by which my soul was able to express itself, to make itself known to me. I began calling upon and listening to my soul. No matter where my soul has taken me, it always has stayed on a righteous path. God has been with me all the way.

Eventually I came to understand that my soul was actually the essence of God within me. I came to understand that at my birth, my soul had actually sought out **me**, the person that I was and would become and the personal events that would shape my life. It was those specifics that would assist my soul in achieving its own spiritual needs, the specific spiritual growth necessary for it to eventually return to God. This is in keeping with what I have been taught.

Don't we all desire to return to God? If only we knew the sure way. Well, the way is through soul growth, and it is the soul within us that guides us along the appropriate and necessary paths. It is the soul within us that returns to God not the personality we inherit while here on Earth.

As I began to think about the role of my soul, to guide me away from less human and toward more godly paths for its own benefit, I again thought of those individuals who lived in the most remote areas of the earth who would never learn of Jesus or of God. Even more disturbing to me was the thought of those persons/souls who died young due to accident or disease and of babies who die before they have even begun to experience life. It is only fair that all souls have equal opportunity to grow. It was then that the idea of reincarnation found its way into my tucker bag of possible and plausible realities. The idea of many lives, many opportunities suddenly became a rational idea for me.

As I continued to read about and ponder reincarnation, another reality presented itself. Not only should all have an equal number of opportunities but opportunities of an equal quality. Thus, if one has endured a life of poverty, another of financial comfort would have been earned; one life of ill health would reap the reward of another of robust health; one life as a man then another life as a woman; one as a member of a minority or downtrodden race then another as a privileged one. Of course, the opposite is true; that is, one life rich another life poor, etc.

For most of us, the memory of past lives is erased in any given lifetime. This is because certain past lifetimes have not been pleasant or admirable.

Some have been tortured and some abominable. Remember, just as we have been good, we've been bad. And just as we have led a happy, healthy, comfortable life, we have led lives of misery. Many of our past lives would be too unpleasant, too unbearable to recall, so God has been kind and allowed us to forget. Occasionally though, little snippets of distant memories creep into our consciousness. We have already mentioned *déjà vu*. We have all experienced that.

I have no memory of any of my past lives with regard to specific names or dates with the exception of the "knowledge" that I was aboard the Titanic. I was a survivor and am inclined to believe that I was a small child. My sister was there, but she was not as fortunate as I. I also "know" that in a lifetime probably just prior to the Titanic experience, I was a man, a native American of the Mescalero tribe living in the foothills of the Rockies in New Mexico, specifically near what is now a very small settlement by the name of Mayhill and another named Weed. The reason that I "know" this is that I spent two summers of my life there at a Girl Scout camp named Camp of the Tall Pines.

When I was in college, I ducked out of summer classes and headed west for summer jobs with the Girl Scouts. I did this for five summers. The first three were spent at Camp Timberlake outside of Fort Worth, Texas, near the "town" of Azle, which everyone said meant "jackass." I don't know about that, but Azle provided three very good cooks, sweet little ladies who came to the camp and cooked for more than one hundred hungry campers and staff. The last two summers were spent at Camp of the Tall Pines not too far from the small ski attraction of Cloudcroft, New Mexico. The area is into the mountains just above the town of Alamogordo and the White Sands missile testing range. Once above the dry, flat areas, the terrain is mountainous and the roads curve after curve, quite foreign to any environment I had experienced. I fell in love with the wooded, mountainous area in which the camp was located. Our camp was near another Girl Scout camp named Camp Mary White, which coincidently was my name at that time. There is a story there but it is not for this writing.

Tall Pines was situated in a small sloping valley formed by a mountain ridge on either side and completely surrounded by pine forests with the exception of one dirt road coming in from the highway. There were no homesteads or settlements for miles. Even though the forest was thick, there were small clearings here and there, which tantalizingly beckoned me to "Come this way. Come and see where I can take you."

I did a lot of exploring on my own mostly on foot but occasionally on horseback, which allowed me deeper access into the unknown. But it did not feel like the unknown to me. It felt like home. There are many stories to tell but again, not for this writing.

I found a small boxful of artifacts while there. I found a number of arrowheads and a stone tool of some sort and some pieces of pottery. And it was the most amazing thing; I found an arrowhead and a small cutting tool right together. They were of white stone, the only white ones I found. Each one was artistically carved with serrated edges unlike any of the rough-hewn others. Immediately when I found them, I thought to myself, *Thank goodness. I thought I had lost these.*

Years later, I took my little box of artifacts to school to my science class for the students to enjoy. One of those students relieved me of my collection. I have wished for their return so many times. I have an unrelenting desire to hold those two pieces from my past again.

I had an experience one night that I must relate here. It has nothing to do with reincarnation, but it does speak to one's spiritual nature. One night, I could not get to sleep. I went outside and sat on the step of the above-ground tent. The air was crisp and clear. It caused my skin to tingle. With head in hand, I began to think, and thought gave way to meditation. As I went deeper into myself, I became aware of the silence. I had never experienced such a profound silence. I felt totally surrounded by nothing but silence. As I allowed myself to be embraced within this very deep silence I heard it: the sound of the earth's rotation. I know that is what it was. I burst into tears and into prayer, thanking God for all He has allowed me to experience. Oh, there is so much more. God has so much to tell us and to show us when we stop long enough to listen and to see.

Anyway, due to the familiarity I felt and the comfort I took in my surroundings at Tall Pines, the small pieces of myself that I perceive that I found there, the spiritual moments of insight that found their way to me while there, I fully believe that I was on home ground those two summers. I have been back just once. I need to go again, if not in this lifetime then maybe in the next.

If you have thought that reincarnation is one of those esoteric ideologies belonging exclusively to one of the far eastern religions, you would be incorrect. Reincarnation was accepted in biblical times. Jesus and his disciples casually referred to the idea of having lived before and having been reborn to another life. Recall in *Matthew* 16:13 when Jesus asked his disciples who men thought that he was and they replied:

"*Some say that thou art John the Baptist: Some, Elias; and others, Jeremiah, or one of the prophets.*"

This demonstrates that they believed in being reborn on Earth, but it also demonstrates that they were not versed in the Eastern philosophy or interpretation of reincarnation. John the Baptist had obviously been killed by this point, but he and Jesus were contemporaries. John baptized Jesus, so this particular part of the response has always puzzled me. Nevertheless, it does demonstrate that reincarnation was an accepted philosophy at that time.

In a nutshell, what we have said about reincarnation is that because the duty of the soul is to perfect itself while in human form, and, since for various reasons and circumstances, this is not possible to accomplish in a single lifetime, multiple lifetimes are required. Reincarnation simply means that the soul has been reborn as an infant human being to experience another needed lifetime. Human souls do not return in lesser life forms. The soul carries with it from lifetime to lifetime memories of past lives. We may or may not experience recall of some of these memories. No set number of lifetimes is required. Each soul progresses at its own pace and on its own merit and no other soul can intercede for another. The soul is an integral part of the human animal. It speaks to and guides the human heart and mind. Just listen! Your soul will inform and educate you. Your soul will assist you in your return to God. Reincarnation is for the benefit of the soul. Reincarnation is a blessing to be thankful for.

KARMA

We Reap That Which We Sow

We've all heard it. We've all said it, but do we believe it? We should because it is an absolute fact. Without fail, whatever we sow we will reap. The twist is that not only what we sow here on Earth in our present lifetime will be reaped here on Earth in our present lifetime but in the spiritual realm, the interim, and in our next lifetime on Earth as well.

Here on Earth, positive actions are not always met with positive results. Often negatives follow positives, and positives follow negatives. But that is here on Earth. Upon physical death or transition to the spiritual realm, all of our earthly actions are seen in their true light as either having been positive or negative, regardless of how they were interpreted on Earth. Each time the soul returns to the spiritual realm, it will contemplate its most recent physical existence, catalogue it within the archives of its total physical lives and experiences, and consider what is lacking spiritually and what its next earthly life must entail. This is where selection comes into play. This is where the soul has input into its earthly life and thereby input into its own journey back to God.

Our present lives are the result of the summation of our past lives. Karma is man's own reward/punishment system. Each of us has determined our own rewards and punishments by the way in which we led not only our most recent life or incarnation but distant past lives as well. In each of the various lives we have led, we have determined what we will experience in the present life and future lives. Each of us has determined our lot in life by how our past lives have been lived. It is such a simple concept. You may think that it is not a fair one because we cannot reach back and change or correct the past, but if you think again, it is an ultimately fair one. We can determine our next life's circumstances by the way in which we live the present one. There is really not a lot to be said by way of explaining karma—as we sow so we reap. That's it. You **are** the master of your fate. You are the architect of your next and future lives and the progression of your soul toward its final goal: reunion with God. Proceed accordingly.

FROM THE AUTHOR, PART ONE

Before closing, I want to make a statement that hopefully will ease the minds and hearts of friend and kin, and anyone else that just may have concerns for the salvation of my soul. I was raised in the Southern Baptist tradition, so I know that most of my ideas go against the grain of religious academia, of orthodoxy. Most Christian sects insist that Jesus was God come to Earth. They base this on their belief in the Trinity, that is, God in three persons: the Father, Son, and Holy Ghost. These traditional ideas really nag at my sense of rationale. This does not mean that I do not believe in Jesus or in the role he played and continues to play in the spiritual enlightenment of many souls who would otherwise languish in the clutches of atheism and soul deterioration.

I know that many orthodox Christians must see me as the worst kind of heretic. For so many years now, I have struggled with the fear that because I do not believe in the divinity of Jesus; because I do not believe that Adam was formed of clay and transformed into a flesh and blood being; because I do not believe that all life on Earth, save half a dozen humans, was destroyed in a worldwide flood, I must be a heretic. But I recently became aware of a category of Christian believers that defines me. I am what is known as a gnostic. It's a rather nasty sounding word, but it doesn't have a nasty meaning. Gnosticism means having intuitive understanding or knowledge of spiritual matters. I believe Gnosticism describes my spiritual path, for everything I believe I have gone to God for affirmation. I have listened to my soul for correctness. This is not to say that I have all the correct information or the definitive answers to anything. It simply means that I am on a truth-seeking journey that is slowly providing me with bits of truth while dispelling many, many untruths. There are only two truths that are written in stone as far as I am concerned and that is that God does exist and that there is but one God rather than three. All other supposed religious truths are open to examination and to change as knowledge is gained. We will stop learning only when our souls are reunited with God and all is made known.

At this point, I would like to make clear what my belief concerning Jesus is. And keep in mind it is my belief based on what my soul dictates to me. I have already said that I believe that Jesus is not God. I have presented scripture from the New Testament that I feel makes it clear that he is not God. So what do I believe? I believe that long before the creation of the earth as described in the first chapter of *Genesis*, the soul that would come to inhabit the body of the man Jesus existed as the ultimately enlightened soul who sat at the right hand of God, in other words, the highest evolved soul under God. He was the equivalent of God's son. After thousands of years and under the influence of evil minds and hearts, mankind was sinking into a spiritual abyss. God sent His beloved son, the soul that was to become known as Jesus, onto the earth to awaken mankind to its spiritual nature and restore mankind onto the path of spiritual enlightenment. This beloved son of God gave up his divinity to return to Earth for the benefit of mankind. Upon his physical death, his divinity was restored as his soul was returned to its rightful place at the right hand of God. That's the long and the short of it. God is, God gave His beloved son for the sake and saving of all mankind, the son came and fulfilled his mission, and the son was recalled to his father. His divinity was restored, and his soul—his spiritual self—was returned to its rightful position next to his father and ours, God. That's how simple the story is. All the rest is embellishment based on the memories of his companions and contemporaries, some memories factual, some distorted, some from hearsay, some born of the imagination. Many "facts" concerning Jesus have been presented by those who never knew him but drew upon the stories of others. These then represent the only "proof" of the existence of the man, Jesus. But there is indisputable proof of the positive effect the life and death of this man had on humankind, all humanity, and continues to have and will always have. Jesus is the Christ, a savior among men, a Messiah.

Now let me speak to the validity or authenticity of the Bible from my viewpoint. I believe that all of the events recorded in the Old Testament of the Christian Bible actually took place. I believe none of them are myths, but I do believe that many of them have been misinterpreted. I think it is accurate and honest to say that any contention I have with my religion is not with the Christian faith per se but is with the scribes who transcribed ancient records and the church fathers who have decided what the Bible should contain, and worse, how these contents should be interpreted, and further, have insisted that these interpretations cannot be questioned or changed, ever.

I have researched and determined that the Old Testament writings are so full of accurate numerical data that it is ludicrous to think that the events connected by this data are figments of anyone's imagination or just myths. The Old Testament contents were written over a long period of time by many different writers, and it is folly to think that all the writers could have, even would have conspired together to bring the various dates and events into accord with one another. Timelines given in the book of *Genesis* actually played out perfectly hundreds, even thousands of years later as predicted. So, yes, I believe in the authenticity of the Old Testament commentary and the validity of the events it recounts. It is the interpretation of these events that I question.

Is the Bible the word of God? The Christian portion, the New Testament, most certainly is not. It is the writings of either the apostles or their later ghostwriters. There are too many errors and truly unbelievable events such as the five loaves of bread and two fish feeding five thousand men and the turning of water into wine at a wedding that bother me. I know that with God all things are possible. I know this. And it is possible that Jesus's faith in God allowed him to perform many seeming miracles. But there are limits to what the logical mind can accept. At this point in my spiritual journey, except for the healings, my mind chooses not to accept these stories literally or as reality.

But it is not simply unbelievable stories that tell me that the New Testament is written in the words of men, not God, but the fact that there are so many contradictions surrounding the main events such as the birth of Jesus, Jesus's genealogy, the life of Jesus, etc. Now, what about the Old Testament? Could the Old Testament be the word of God? I think you already know what I have to say about this—NO! I could go on and on as to why in my mind the contents of the Bible were not dictated by God. But I won't.

Traditional Judaism and Christianity, and I think Islam, for that matter, believes that the god of the Old Testament is God the Creator. But that god, the one who came down to Earth and personally, often in human form, had dealings with Adam, Noah, Abraham, Jacob, Moses and all the Old Testament prophets, priests, and kings was an imposter. He gave no thought other than destructive ones to the bulk of mankind that inhabited the earth at that time who were biologically unrelated to the Israelites. This "god" divulged his name to Moses, and his name was Jehovah, and, as he vowed, Jehovah is his name to time indefinite. Even in his absence, (*Genesis*, Chapter 6: "*My spirit shall not act toward man indefinitely . . .*") he continues to fool mankind. I have devoted many pages of commentary and verses of scripture to the debunking of this demigod, this fallible, prideful, vengeful, ineffective, murdering, utterly evil, not of this earth entity. He has duped mankind long enough. Let's hope that he never returns to Earth.

"Never returns to earth." Ah, now we are down to it. I imagine the majority of you is thinking, "This gal's a whack-o!" But then, apparently, the majority of you have not had what is commonly known as a UFO experience.

▷—◁

FROM THE AUTHOR, PART TWO

Imagine this scenario: You are an eleven-year-old boy, and you and your brother are out one night, poking around a home construction site, scavenging for wood scraps with which to build a bicycle ramp. Something catches your attention, and you look up to see an amber-colored object hovering just above the rooftop and as large as the house itself. You manage to gasp, "What is that?" Your brother replies, "What?" but before he can look up, the object zips down to a pinpoint of light and is gone. You and your brother return home, but you are so shaken by the experience that you will not relate it to your parents. In fact, you are so shaken by the experience that you cannot talk of it for several years.

Imagine this scenario: You are an elderly woman who lives in a rural area. You neglected to pick up your mail during the day, so since it is now after dark, you get into your car to make the long drive down your driveway to the mailbox which is situated across the county highway that passes in front of your property. When you reach the end of your driveway, you do not get out of the car because there is an amber-colored sphere the size of a soccer ball hovering over the electrical wires above your mailbox. The wires run parallel to the road. You return to the house and call your nearest neighbor who lives about a quarter of a mile down the road, and she agrees to have you pick her up to come and see the mysterious object. When you again reach the end of the driveway, you make the right-hand turn taking you in the direction of your neighbor's, and the hovering object begins to travel alongside until you reach your neighbor's driveway. You turn left and drive the two hundred yards to her house. She is outside waiting and gets into your car, and you turn around and return to the highway. The object is still hovering there over the electrical wires. You drive back in the direction of your house, and the object moves along beside you. You do not stop at your home but continue driving down the highway. The object continues to move with you. You drive for approximately three miles to the Mississippi/Louisiana state line, and the object continues to travel with you. You turn around and return to your own driveway and stop. The object has returned with you, stops, slowly moves away from the wires and zips to a pinpoint of light and is gone.

Imagine this scenario: You are in your forties, sitting in your living room watching the ten o'clock local news on the television when the following is announced: "We interrupt to report that Officer _____ of the Harrison County Sheriff's Department is at this moment in pursuit of an unidentified flying object. The object is moving westward along Highway 53 toward Hancock County."

That's barely a mile from you, so you jump up, call for all family members, and you all go outside onto the pool deck behind your house, which puts you facing due west toward Hancock County. Your view of the sky is completely unobstructed. Low in the sky you see an amber-colored sphere resembling in color and appearance the headlights of an airplane approaching from a good distance away. You have seen this many times before. The others return to the house but you remain. As you continue to watch, you realize that as this light approaches, you are not beginning to see red and green pulsing lights or hearing the sound of an airplane's jet engines. Then you realize, it is not approaching you but is traveling along a due south path, which will take it toward the Gulf of Mexico. You continue to watch until it becomes just a flicker of light, and you are just barely able to keep it in view. You think to yourself, *Shoot! It must be over the water by now,* meaning about ten to twelve miles south of you.

As you thought this to yourself, to your amazement the object begins to become clearer. You hold your breath. Unbelievably, it is coming back and in your direction which is due northeast. The object had not turned or banked. It simply changed direction as though it had just stopped in midair and reset its course. You realize it is coming directly toward you. As it gets closer, you walk away from the house into an open area that was once a small garden. The object comes to a stop directly above you. You have to lay your head back as far as you can in order to view it. By now, it is the size of your thumbnail when held at arm's length. You cannot tell how high up the object is but you estimate fifty yards. Its light does not flicker or pulse. The object is static. There is no movement and there is no sound.

As you continue to watch, you think of saying to "them": *You want information from me, but you are not willing to give me information.* When your neck can no longer endure the strain, you return to the pool area, and as you continue to watch, you become aware of one of your sons standing behind a shrub. You ask your son to go and retrieve your binoculars, but he replies, "I want to see too." You go into the house for the binoculars and return in less than two minutes to see the object drifting away barely above the tops of the pine trees and now headed in a southeasterly direction.

There were three related individuals involved in these experiences that spanned a period of over thirty years and what they will all tell you is that the experience was real, not imagined. But that is all that they can tell you. They do not know what they experienced. The only proof they have is the reality of the situation that is forever embedded in their minds. Other than the memory, they are left only with the perpetual desire to know and understand exactly what they witnessed. And, yes, I am one of those witnesses.

It is obvious that the experiences cannot be explained away as natural phenomena. They cannot be glibly explained away as supernatural experiences. There was no lost time, no blacking out of the memory, no displacement of bodies.

(Speaking of displacement of bodies, I had occasion to personally meet and speak with Charles Hickson, one of two men who, in 1973, claimed to have been teleported into a hovering craft from the Pascagoula River where they were fishing. In my estimation, Mr. Hickson was totally sincere and genuine. If you would like to read of his experience, try looking on Google, "Remembering Charlie Hickson"/Open Minds TV).

Going back to the experiences recounted here, what we have to agree on is that the objects seen by these people were being intelligently controlled. So what! We know that the United States government has many secret projects dealing with very advanced processes, really phenomenal, unbelievable feats. This is true, but it begs the question, "Does the U.S. government have nothing better or more important to do than the nighttime stalking of ordinary people going about their ordinary lives?" And how many thousands of individuals worldwide have reported similar experiences and even more traumatic ones? Is alien visitation and intervention for real? Only time will tell. Does the Bible suggest alien intervention? I believe it does.

I said to the man
Who stood at the gate of the year,
"Give me a light that I may
Tread safely into the unknown."
And he replied,
"Go into the darkness
And put your hand
Into the hand of God.
That shall be to you
Better than light
And safer than a known way."

—Minnie Louise Haskin
1908

www.ingramcontent.com/pod-product-compliance
Lightning Source LLC
Chambersburg PA
CBHW031427290426
44110CB00011B/556